Two Scoops of Grace with Chuckles on Top:

Sweet, Funny Reminders of God's Heart for You

Jeanette Levellie

Illustration
Ron Leve

Lighthouse Publishing
of the Carolinas

Contents

Where's the Bull?	7
Enjoy Your Noodles	11
Why Not Me?	15
The Reluctant Preacher's Wife	19
Crawzilla	23
Can Preachers Have Sex on Sundays?	27
Embarrassing Moments	31
God Isn't	35
Revenge of the Remote Control	39
The Pact	43
The Biggest Trophy	47
I'm Behind You	51
Cow Chip Classic	55
Keepers	59
God's Logic	63
Do What You Can	67
From Hair to Eternity	71
Adventures in Fasting	75
I Believe in Blabbing	79
Honest to God	83
Ice Cream Snatcher	87
Do You Want a Spanking?	91
Honey, Have You Seen My Teeth?	95
The Divine No	99
Not Kleenex, Tissues	103
What, No Worm? (Candy's Apples)	107
The Unrepentant Kitten	111
I Don't Mind	115
Secret Offerings	119
Help Me!	123
The Brouhaha Twins	127
Jumping Bales with Jesus	131
A Radical Secret for Forgiving Sister Sourpuss and Brother Barracuda	135
The Grave of the Unknown Cat	139
Take a Closer Look	143
A Hairy Deal	147

The Empty Box	151
Baby Plans	155
Beware of Moths and Sligs	159
The Hormone Bomber	163
Buttons	167
The Christmas Wedding Hero	171
My Un-favorite Characters	175
The Surprising Yellow Smile	179
Drive-by Diapers	183
Let My Conscience Be Your Guide	187
I Don't Care What Boo-Boo Thinks	191
NO Is Not a Four-letter Word	195
I've Fallen Off the Pedestal and I Refuse to Climb Back Up	199
Tomorrow's Menu	203
Time to Be God's Baby	207
God's Tattoo	211
Ditzy? Maybe. Stupid? Never!	215
You Love Me	219
Dings and Beeps	223
Be Somebody	227
Estie and Uncle Ken	231
Minor Alterations	235
Sticks, Stones, and Words that Wound	239
Culture Shock	243
Sharing My Messes	247
Farmer Girl	251
Dangerous Donuts	255
From Outlaws to God's Kids	259
Who Are You Laughing At?	263
Wrinkles and All	267
Just Give Me a Kiss	271
Leave Yourself Alone	275
Not My Thought	279
A Pitiful Slice of Pie	283
No Charge	287
The Rest of Your Life	291
Thank You for Changing My Destiny	295

To Kevin

My Hero, My Best Friend, My Lover

Thanks for showing,
not just telling, Jesus.

Where's the Bull?

"Therefore let us draw near with confidence to the throne of grace, so that we may receive mercy and find grace to help in time of need"
(Hebrews 4:16 NASB).

"Animal Control?"

"Yes, this is Austin at Animal Control."

"My name is Jeanette Levellie. I live at 775 Engle Avenue, in front of the Christian Church. A bull is running loose in our backyard! Please come quickly!"

"All right, ma'am, we'll have someone there right away."

"Hurry, please," I choked through panicky tears. Then I called Kevin.

"Honey, a bull from next door has broken through our fence! Can't you do something? I called Animal Control, but they haven't arrived yet."

"I'll be right there, sweetheart. Don't panic."

Sitting on the edge of the bed, I tried to pray through the sobs. We'd only been married a few months. Our recent move to a suburb of Santa Maria on the California coast excited us. The two and a half acres our church and parsonage sat on felt like a ranch to us city kids. At first, we had thought it sweet that the Catholic priests at the rectory next door allowed 4-H'ers to keep their animal projects in their pasture. Now I wondered if crazy was a better word to describe their neighborliness.

My imagination running amuck, I envisioned the headline: "Twenty-year-old Minister's Wife Mauled by Runaway Bull." Although I'd never met a bull in person, I'd seen enough movies to know if you came anywhere near one, especially if you were wearing red, you'd better get right with God.

"Where's the bull?" the Animal Control men asked when Kev answered the doorbell. He bravely led them around to the backyard. They were ready with large sticks, to protect themselves in case the bull decided to charge, and to herd it back to its own yard. These men were heroes in my eyes. I was already planning the letter to the editor I would write in their honor.

But when I ran to the back bedroom and peeked through the curtains to see the action, they stood with their clubs in limp hands, heads thrown back, guffawing. They weren't even trying to corral that bull. What was wrong with them?

When Kevin returned to the house, he explained the men's behavior. Through tears of amusement, they'd said, "This isn't a bull. It's a year-old heifer. Does someone around here belong to 4-H?"

Kev told them how we, unfamiliar with livestock, thought it was a bull when we saw the horns. This led to more laughter, and they promised to rescue us as they slipped a rope around the gentle animal's neck.

Although I was embarrassed at my naiveté, I was relieved we were safe. I rushed outside to have my photo taken with the wandering "bull" before they led him home.

Many situations in my life that I thought were bulls turned out to be only heifers. Deceived by the enemy, not knowing God's Word well enough to understand His power and love, I often cried to the Lord, "Help; I'm in danger!" Although God is too polite to laugh at my panic, He always rescued me from my troubles. But I could have avoided many embarrassing moments if I'd put my trust in Him sooner.

Don't let Satan convince you that whatever mess you are experiencing is a bull that will ruin your life and shatter your dreams. God says, "Nothing is impossible to those who believe." Keep your eyes on His goodness and willingness to turn the toughest circumstances around. Look for promises in His Word that assure you of His faithfulness, and respectfully remind Him of them.

You'll soon be watching those "bulls" run for the pasture. And you'll be the one laughing. At the devil.

Two Scoops & a Sprinkle
- ❖ Asking for help from others or the Lord should not embarrass us. Even if I'd known about the heifer, I could not have corralled it back to its pen without help.
- ❖ Boldness in prayer and bossing God isn't the same. God invites us to ask boldly for the help we need. He doesn't get mad at us when we remind Him of His promises. It honors Him to rescue us.
- ❖ What fun to look back and laugh at ourselves over silly mistakes we've made that at the time seemed like crises. Finding the humor in our foibles relaxes us, and endears us to others.

Enjoy Your Noodles

"Be content with what you have, because God has said, 'Never will I leave you; never will I forsake you'"
(Hebrews 13:5b NIV).

The sign on the counter clinched my decision: "Our chicken stew voted one of America's Top 10 Best Chicken Dishes by *Redbook* magazine." My imagination salivated: plump chicken breast slices bumped into carrots; potato and celery chunks jostled for position to the top of the bowl, showing off their muscles.

It was our first visit to this highly celebrated deli recommended by our friend, James. We'd taken three wrong turns before we finally found it. But when we opened the door and breathed in the aromas of fresh-baked bread, deli meats, and kosher dills, my frustration vanished.

While a smiling server behind the counter ladled out my stew, I congratulated myself on my healthy selection, compared to my husband's choice of a pastrami sandwich. Until I stared into my bowl.

Nothing but noodles.

Okay, that was a lie. Scraps of chicken and a slice or two of carrot hid next to scrawny excuses for celery. Apart from that, the noodle family and their 106 noodle cousins swam in a lake of broth.

Kevin charged into his five-inch mound of pastrami on rye, the spicy mustard dripping onto his moustache to mock me.

"How is your sandwich, honey?"

"It's great! I'm so glad we came here, Jeanette." He wiped his mouth between bites. "It was worth all the trouble of finding it. You know, there aren't many places that serve pastrami like this anymore. And just look how they piled it on."

How could he manage to get all those words out and all that food in at the same time? "I'm thankful to James for recommending this restaurant. Would you like a bite?"

"Oh, no, that's okay." I pretended not to mind that his taste buds were dancing in pastrami heaven while mine languished in . . . well.

His eyes closed in bliss while he took another bite. "How is your stew?"

"I would hardly call it stew," I whined. "I expected tons of veggies and huge chunks of chicken. This is barely more than a bowl of noodles splashed with chicken, and carrots tossed in for color." I kept my voice calm despite the stress of my enormous disappointment, so he wouldn't feel bad.

I needn't have worried. No amount of discontent on my part could quench his pastrami-induced joy.

After fishing each sliver of chicken and hint of veggie from the pond of noodles—while listening to the virtues of the Best Pastrami on Earth between slabs of the freshest rye in the universe—I excused myself. *Perhaps on my way to the ladies room I'll happen by a table recently vacated by people who left half a sandwich untouched. I can sneak it into my purse and then eat it behind the stall door—with a napkin on my lap, of course. I'm no lowbrow, after all.*

But my conscience—and the empty plates I passed—made my decision for me. It seems the Lord had taken seriously my plea of "lead me not into temptation" when I prayed that morning.

While alone in the bathroom, I silently complained to the Lord about my stew. As He often does when my attitude is tacky, He spoke to me. I didn't hear an audible voice, but way down on the inside of my insides, I sensed His kind, Daddy tone.

"Enjoy your noodles," He said. As flat and matter-of-fact as someone saying, "Here's a napkin to wipe your chin."

I blinked. *Well, of course. This is what I have in my bowl. Just because I expected a different meal, doesn't mean I can't enjoy these noodles. I should be happy for food in my belly, not miffed because I didn't get my way.*

I returned to the table, inspired by my little bathroom talk with Jesus, and slurped down the remainder of my lunch. I grinned at Kevin and said, "This deli was an excellent choice.

Thanks for paying, honey."

"You're welcome."

Even his pastrami breath didn't faze me. Too much.

Two Scoops & a Sprinkle

❖ Unrealistic expectations can keep us from enjoying a meal, a relationship, or the place God has us.

❖ Attitudes are powerful. They can break your spirit or make your day. The good news is, all it takes to change one is a little, inside adjustment.

❖ When we share a meal with someone we love, what we have on our plate isn't the main course.

Why Not Me?

"Since God has so generously let us in on what he is doing, we're not about to throw up our hands and walk off the job just because we run into occasional hard times"
(2 Corinthians 4:1 The Message).

When I picked up the phone after supper, I heard, "Want to go for a walk? I gained five pounds on vacation, Ginger needs to exercise, and Bob is working tonight. I hate to walk alone."

It was just like my neighbor Lacy to plunge right into the conversation without identifying herself. That was okay with me, though. I'd have known that sweet-as-taffy soprano anywhere. Even on the rare occasions when she said, "I'm feeling kind of down," it came out like a song.

"Okay," I answered. "Let me put my tennies on, and I'll meet you out front in five minutes."

The sun was starting to finger paint on the horizon. Pink swirled with mauve and orange made a happy background for our conversation. Lacy's poodle Ginger skittered ahead on her extra long leash, sniffing every second bush. Soon we found ourselves near Lacy's Uncle Jay's house.

Lacy waved a pudgy hand at her uncle as he sat on his front porch swing. "How are you doing, Jay?" she sang out.

Uncle Jay narrowed his eyes to focus. "Oh, it's you," he hollered across the huge lawn. "Walk on the other side of the street, if you don't mind. The last time you came down my sidewalk, I had to pay a week's salary to get the cracks repaired. They don't make heavy-duty sidewalks in this town, you know!"

We rolled our eyes and laughed, pretending to be amused. Then Lacy whispered to me, "Watch this." While her uncle rambled on about the price of sidewalk repairs, Lacy bent down to scratch Ginger's ears, apparently sharing a secret with her.

I couldn't hear what she said, but as soon as Lacy stood up, Ginger squatted down and pooped, right in Uncle Jay's yard.

My mouth fell to my shoes. "What did you tell that dog?" I demanded.

"To poop right there," Lacy said. "Jay won't even find it until he comes out to mow on the weekend. Besides, he deserves it for calling me fat!"

She scooted off toward home, Ginger trotting ahead. Although I couldn't argue with her, I wondered how my front yard would look if, every time I acted ornery, someone brought their pooch to poop on my lawn. My guess was, not much grass would be showing.

Sometimes, however, I think I don't deserve the poops that

come my way. A dear friend makes a remark that slices a piece from my heart. I experience a huge disappointment. Someone I trusted betrays a confidence. A dream lies broken and smashed.

Or my favorite uncle calls me fat.

As I'm tempted to wallow in pity, I think, "Why should I be exempt from poops? Everyone else has problems, some much larger than mine. What makes me think I'm so special that I can avoid trouble? Why should my yard be the only perfect one?"

I live on a damaged planet. I shouldn't be shocked when poops happen. Instead of asking, "Why me, Lord?" I'd be wiser to ask, "Why not me?" then go out and try to improve someone else's life. Perhaps if I concentrated on helping them clean up their poops, deserved or not, the whole neighborhood would smell sweeter.

Make that the whole world.

Two Scoops & a Sprinkle

❖ We can always find someone else in worse circumstances than our own. Visiting a nursing home or talking to an unemployed neighbor may put our problems into perspective.

❖ When someone insults you, try praying for him or her instead of retaliating. If you want to shock them into silence, take their hand and pray for them aloud.

❖ We can make the world a sweeter place by refusing to dwell on the poops. What creative ways can we improve a sour situation?

The Reluctant Preacher's Wife

"The Lord will fulfill his purpose for me; your love, O Lord, endures forever—do not abandon the works of your hands"
(Psalm 138:8 NIV).

"Yes—he wants to meet my parents!" My heart spun in circles. A secret crush, Ethan, had asked to accompany me home from college Easter weekend.

Kevin Levellie, another friend of Ethan's, pastored a small church in Fresno, where my folks lived. After Sunday evening worship, Ethan and I popped over to Kevin's house, visiting into the night. Driving back to school the next morning, Ethan suggested we pray for Kevin. Seems he thought a wife would cure Kevin's loneliness.

Eager to impress Ethan I nearly sang, "All right! I'll go first."

"Dear Lord, please lead a woman into Kevin's life who will stand beside him, offering hope in the darkness and laughter in the bright times, who will help him pastor your sheep with tenderness, bringing out the best in him and them. In Jesus' name, Amen."

Shortly after my show-offy prayer, Ethan lost interest in me. Although confused and hurt, I accepted his explanation that he felt inferior because I had wheels and he didn't.

That spring, Kevin and I started writing. This old-fashioned custom requires use of a pen and paper to tell someone what's been going on in your life, and ask him about his. After finishing the *letter,* you fold the paper, place it in an envelope, attach a stamp, and mail it. Archaic, I know, but effective.

When I returned home for the summer, our friendship soared. By August, my ring finger danced in the Fresno sun, clad in a diamond bikini.

Before the wedding, I imagined marriage to Kev as one eternal Bible study, with meals in between. *When I come home from work at night, we'll sit for hours discussing spiritual matters. If Kevin becomes disheartened over issues at church, I'll encourage him and send him back out to the battle with renewed confidence.* It never entered my naive brain what kinds of circumstances might cause him pain.

After thirty-plus years of marriage, I confess we've engaged in as many battles as Bible studies. Our conversations haven't always been pleasant or spiritual. And I've needed as much or more cheerleading as Kevin has.

Do God's methods of answering prayer baffle you? Although I consider myself creative, I did not have *me* in mind when I asked God to send Kevin a wife. In fact, I had insisted since childhood that a preacher was my last choice as a spouse because I wanted to be rich.

To complicate things further, you won't find me on the cover of *Ideal Pastor's Wife Weekly*. I never learned to play piano. If I did play, it would be too loud for older folks, and I'd invent my own rhythm. A time or two, I have argued with my husband in the middle of a sermon. I once shocked the entire congregation with my choice of Easter attire.

And my house? It's the global convention center for cobwebs. I refuse to cook a recipe with more than five ingredients, and I sweep the kitchen floor by sliding across it in my stocking feet. Every bed and recliner has its own cat, whom I treat like children in fur suits.

Yet, in spite of my numerous faults and unconventional ways, God blessed me with a man I love and admire. Oh, and he happens to be a preacher. Who am I to look the Great I Am in the face and say, "You bungled it the day you called me, Lord. I'm too silly, loud, impulsive, and messy to make a decent pastor's wife."

He would only smile and say, "You asked for a wife for Kevin, didn't you?"

Two Scoops & a Sprinkle

❖ Allowing God to change your dreams brings a wealth of joy.

❖ Get rid of preconceived notions about marriage, a career, or the ministry. Things are never as you expect they will be.

❖ You don't have to fit a certain mold to minister effectively to people. God loves variety. He wants to use you exactly as He created you.

Crawzilla

"The Lord does not look at the things man looks at. Man looks at the outward appearance, but the Lord looks at the heart" **(1 Samuel 16:7 NIV).**

Our first spring in Paris, Illinois found us settled into country living better than we'd expected. Or so I imagined. A lifetime in a city of five million can't prepare you for the crazy things that happen in a rural town.

One morning I was up before the sun. The predawn sky was gray and still. I hadn't inhaled any caffeine yet, so my brain was fuzzy when I opened the back door to let the cats in. But what I saw creeping across the lawn woke me up fast. I charged down the hall to our bedroom, adrenaline taking over.

"Kev, get up, *now*," I shrieked, flapping my hands in front of me. "There's a huge insect out back, bigger than any I've seen in my life! It's even uglier than those horrible potato bugs we had in California. It has enormous claws, and it's waving them in the air. Hurry, it's going to get the kitties!"

My husband doesn't function well if jolted from a deep sleep at any hour. Add a frantic redhead shouting about a killer insect, and you multiply his perplexity. He creaked up, slowly reaching for his glasses, and scratched his head.

By this time, I was sobbing, wringing my hands. "Honey, *please*. Go squish that horrible thing before it attacks my kitties!" I rushed to the back door and flung it open. In my wide-screen imagination, I saw my babies sprawled on the lawn, stiff from the poisonous pinch of this science-fiction-like creature.

After an eon or so, Kev stumbled down the hall and out the door, peering onto the lawn to view this potential murderer of my cats. He let his eyes adjust to the dim light for a few minutes while I stood whimpering beside him. Then his chuckling started. A soft, baby chuckle at first, growing to a hearty guffaw fit for an emperor.

"Jeanette, do you know what this is?"

I wiped tears from my face. "No, but can't you just kill it?"

"Honey, this is a *crawdad*. It must have crawled up from the creek when it rained last night. It will find its way back, and it's more afraid of your cats than they are of it. Let's go in and make some coffee."

He couldn't help shaking his head at my city-bred naiveté. I suppose I did panic a little, but never having seen a crawdad before, it sure looked like an enormous killer insect to me!

Kev still teases me about the morning he rescued my fur babies from "Crawzilla." I laugh, too. Until I think about how our lives brim with human Crawzillas.

What if I mistook a person as I did that insect, believing the gossip someone told me about them, then judged them based on rumors? Would I treat them differently than if I "believed the best of every person" as Paul directs in I Corinthians 13?

Do we laugh about our mistakes in misjudging crawdads, but think it's okay to judge people by their appearance, their occupation, or their name? I once heard a preacher say, "You know you are free of prejudice when you treat someone who can do you absolutely no good as well as you treat someone who has the ability to greatly help you."

That's how Jesus lived. He hung out with prostitutes, IRS agents, and filthy fishermen. He was willing to look beyond the surface and offer people a chance to be His friends regardless of what stereotypes others placed on them.

If I treat certain people worse than others because they look undesirable or have a poor reputation, I'm not operating God's way. He looks on the heart. That's enough for Him. It should be enough for me, too, since I'm His child.

You are still not going to catch me dancing with crawdads in the early morning hours, or opening the door before I've had my coffee. But Crawzilla taught me that you can't judge a creature by his cover.

Two Scoops & a Sprinkle

❖ We all know people who appear unfriendly, stupid, or arrogant when we first meet them. As we get to know them beneath the surface of their insecurities, we find likable individuals. The saying "First impressions count" does not apply to discerning, love-motivated believers.

❖ Believing the best of others not only means refusing to criticize them verbally; it also means curbing judgmental thoughts about them, and praying for them instead.

❖ Did you ever wonder what your first impression of Jesus would be if He showed up in our world today?

Can Preachers Have Sex on Sundays?

"Come, my beloved, let us go out into the country"
(Song of Solomon 7:11 NASB).

When our son, Ron, was in his preteen "girls are gross" stage, the word *breast* embarrassed him. For several months, I accommodated him by calling chicken breasts "chicken chests" when I served them for dinner. In my opinion, using a different name drew attention to them, but I was trying to respect his modesty.

A few people are not so respectful of intimate issues. As we were leaving a party one Saturday night, someone asked me what we were going to do the next day.

"Oh, the usual," I replied. *What do preachers usually do on Sundays?* I thought.

The wannabe comedian then asked, "Can preachers have sex on Sundays?"

"Sure," I said, "as long as it's with their spouse." *And if the kids aren't home.*

When our kids were toddlers, the friends in Mr. Rogers' Neighborhood made great babysitters from time to time. On rare occasions, we saved up for a special night in a nearby motel. Relatives kept the kids overnight, and we felt like honeymooners. When Esther and Ron were old enough to stay alone a few hours, we'd sneak off for a drive at dusk, then park somewhere to sit and talk. And other stuff.

One night we were not doing any other stuff, simply visiting. I was clear over on my side of the seat, leaned against the passenger door, facing Kevin. We'd chosen a quiet, industrial neighborhood to park in, so few cars passed.

Suddenly, a police officer stood at Kevin's window, his flashlight targeting our faces. Kevin's hand trembled as he rolled down the window.

"Yes?" he managed to croak.

"I saw you sitting here, and thought I'd check to see that everything is all right." The officer leaned down to make eye contact with me. "You okay, ma'am?"

"Yes, I'm fine. We were only talking." I gulped.

"Okay, just wanted to be certain. No problems? You sure?" His gaze held mine again, his eyes serious but kind.

Hoping he didn't notice my face turning the same color as the light on his patrol car, I nodded and smiled. That seemed to satisfy him, and off he roared.

The following day, I called the Los Angeles police department, thanking them for their conscientiousness. I explained how protected I felt the previous night. The sergeant in charge was shocked.

"Most people resent it when a patrolman checks on them, and they call to complain about the invasion of privacy."

"Well, we were parked in an industrial district. That's not exactly private. And the officer who questioned us did not know we were married, and just needed to get away from our kids for a while!" He chuckled appreciatively. I'll bet he had kids of his own.

After we hung up, I grinned in satisfaction. *I love making someone's day*, I thought. Then a great idea zipped by: *Maybe I'll invite him and his wife over for dinner one night. I'll serve them my special recipe of chicken chests.*

Two Scoops & a Sprinkle

❖ It's okay that your older kids know you enjoy an intimate relationship, as long as you set boundaries on how much they know. TMI (too much information) can be unhealthy for children and teens.

❖ Finding creative ways to get off alone adds pizzazz to your marriage.

❖ Turning off the phone at certain times is a way to show your spouse that they take priority over work and friends. If you allow calls any time of day or night, your sex life may suffer.

My Secret Recipe for Chicken Chests:

4 boneless skinless chicken chest halves (1 lb.)

1 cup Italian salad dressing

2 Tablespoons grated Parmesan cheese

1 cup Italian seasoned croutons, crushed

Place chicken in a greased 9-inch-square baking dish. Drizzle with salad dressing. Roll in crushed croutons, and sprinkle with cheese. Bake, uncovered, at 375 degrees for 20-25 minutes or until chicken juices run clear. Yield: 4 servings.

Embarrassing Moments

*"For the Lamb at the center of the throne will be their
shepherd; he will lead them to springs of living water. And God
will wipe away every tear from their eyes"*
(Revelation 7:17 NIV).

It's good I don't embarrass easily because I often fill my days
with ditziness. I never took a class in Ditziness. It just comes
along with the red hair. I'm okay with it. I like myself. I even
laugh at my own jokes, whether you join in or not.

A few times in my life, though, I have humiliated myself.
Once it concerned farm machinery.

When we relocated from Los Angeles to Illinois, I knew
nothing about farming. I thought a corncrib was a baby bed
made from corncobs. The first time I saw bales of hay in a field,
I asked what those huge round "thingies" were. And I could not
figure out why all the roads had ditches on either side!

While working at the front desk of Citizens Bank one smoky October day shortly after moving to Illinois, I noticed a young mother with her small son. He couldn't have been older than three. When I spoke to him, he inched over to my desk, clutching a brightly painted farm toy. I like kids, so he must have sensed a friend in me.

As we talked, he wheeled his beloved farm toy around my pencil holder, over my photo frames, and down my monitor. I imagined him falling asleep that night with his sweaty little fingers hugging the toy's bright green belly.

Running out of conversation topics, I looked down at his toy and remarked, "I like your tractor." It seemed like a kind, friendly thing to say in the middle of a kind, friendly talk. I was unprepared when the pride of fifty-seven generations of farming family exploded from this indignant preschooler: "It's not a tractor. *It's a combine!*"

Opening my mouth to make a witty retort, I managed only a wimpy "Oh, really?" All my city smarts and computer knowledge were worthless when it came to identifying a farm toy. I had been bested by a baby. He tromped off to find his mom, no doubt muttering, "What kind of grownup is she?"

I would have quit right then, if I wasn't so used to my paycheck. Or at least gone home with a paper sack over my head. The best I could do was hope to never again see Mister "It's-Not-A-Tractor."

What a relief to know the lovely place I'll be living forever has no embarrassment in it. My personal theory is that we will spend the first fifty trillion years looking at DVDs of everyone's life—with all the bad parts edited out. We will only view the victories.

No mistaken identity of farm equipment. No sins. No poverty, sickness, or fear. The King and the Lamb banished all those on Resurrection morning.

What abounds there are only the loving, faithful things we've done. Every word you've spoken to comfort and encourage a friend in trouble. All your kind, unselfish acts. The many times you pointed young people in the right direction. The examples of integrity and hard work you've set for your kids. The sacrifices you made of precious time and valuables. Grace. Healing. Joy. The only true utopia.

If you're not sure how to get there, please ask me how. I promise, I won't be a bit embarrassed to tell you.

Two Scoops & a Sprinkle

❖ Embarrassment can be a good thing if it causes us to see a fault we need to correct. But if we embarrass too easily, it may be a sign that we think we're above making mistakes.

❖ When we dwell on the beauty and joy of our heavenly home, it helps make the troubles of this short life fade a little.

❖ Time lends perspective. Although I felt stupid when a three-year-old corrected me, I can laugh about it now.

God Isn't

"Jesus said to her, 'I who speak to you am He'"
(John 4:26 NASB).

My husband has preached an entire sermon atop a ladder, while I fervently prayed in the pew below. He has dressed up as numerous crazy characters, covered the center aisle with coats on Palm Sunday, and used his old teddy bear as a prop. Creativity is his strong suit.

One of his most clever methods to illustrate God's character is to teach us how He *doesn't* behave:

"Does God condemn sinners, sending them away to rot in their misery? No. He lifts them out of their sin by taking their place, redeeming them from death." Or, "Does God rebuke us when we boldly ask Him for a miracle, like the Syrophoenecian woman did? No. He admires our faith and tenacity."

Since Kevin's my husband, I knew he would forgive me if I stole his idea. So I looked back on my journey of faith, especially our years in ministry, and discovered some surprises about my Father. He discloses His heart to us by saying "I AM NOT" as much as when He declares "I AM." Have you discovered this too?

God isn't . . .

. . . worried

The Good Shepherd is not afraid that if the economy fails, He won't be able to supply your needs. His provision is based on His riches (Philippians 4:19), not global events or your employment status. Heaven is off-limits to recession and depression. If you are God's child and you're a tither, He has promised to care for you. He won't become angry if you are bold enough to remind Him of that promise. I think it would honor the Lord that you are coming to Him instead of the government or Uncle Charlie.

. . . tired

When you approach your Father, asking the same favor for the three hundredth time, He doesn't say, "Oh, you again? I have more important people and things to manage today." He longs to have mercy on you and show you favor. He rises to have compassion on you (Isaiah 30:18). Jesus said, "If you, a mere earthly father, will give good things to your kids, how much more will your Heavenly Father give to those who ask Him?"

. . . offended

The Master of the universe doesn't feel insulted when ungodly people take His name in vain, refuse to believe in Him, or twist His Word around to suit their narrow perceptions. It doesn't distress Him if people try to explain creation by theories or attempt to prove He doesn't exist. In fact, He laughs at them (Psalm 2:4). But, I do sometimes wonder if He cringes when His kids act worse than heathens, fighting among themselves. That may tick Him off. . . .

. . . stupid

The God of all wisdom knows more than all of us put together. I know it's laughable to see it in print. Then, why do we seek His guidance as Plan Z instead of A? Why do we trust people's word over His? He has all the direction we will ever need. When we ask, He promises to share (James 1:5). And don't think He only speaks in church on Sunday morning between nine thirty and noon through a trained preacher. Open your Bible some Tuesday afternoon or Saturday morning, and see what's happening in His heart.

. . . religious

The Lord of creation loves to surprise us by solving things His way, rather than how we've figured it out. He used a pimple-faced, sweaty teenager to kill a giant who had an entire army terrified. What unconventional method might He use to fix your problem?

Two Scoops & a Sprinkle

❖ When we impose our own ideas on how God should rescue us from dilemmas, we limit our ability to receive surprises from Him. He loves to astonish His children with His toolkit of miracles. Opening our hearts and saying, "Okay, God, do it your way," frees our thinking to expect a miracle or two.

❖ We may come to God as often as we like and need, reminding Him of His many promises to us. His storehouses of patience and mercy never run out. It blesses Him to bless us.

❖ If we make prayer the first item on our agenda instead of the last resort, we won't stumble around in the dark as often.

Revenge of the
Remote Control

"Are you so foolish? After beginning with the Spirit, are you now trying to attain your goal by human effort?"
(Galatians 3:3 NIV).

It should have been a simple evening: watch an old black-and-white movie, munch some popcorn, and forget about car troubles for a couple of hours. We'd just settled onto the sofa, though, when pandemonium struck.

"Can you turn it up, Hon? I can't hear the dialogue."

Kev reached for the remote. It wasn't between the sofa cushions, on the arm of his recliner, or on top of the TV.

"There it is, on that stack of books next to the turntable." I tried to be kind, even though we'd missed the first three minutes already, and would have to wind it back.

"No, that's the remote for the VCR. We want the one for the TV."

"Oh. Is that it, on your desk there?"

"No, that's for the CD player."

"How many remotes do you have, anyway?"

"Five."

"Good grief! We could write the screenplay to a new movie by the time we find the correct remote, just to turn the volume up. Why can't you simply walk over to the TV and turn it up manually?"

"I could, but that wouldn't solve the problem of the lost remote. I know it's around here somewhere. I just used it this morning. . . ."

"I'm going to California to visit my mother. Let me know when you find it," I said. No little gadget was going to steal my peace, but we humans sure like to complicate things with our myriad inventions.

There was a time when Christianity was simple. You came up out of the baptismal waters glowing. Afterward, you were so grateful for your new life, all you could do was smile, sing, and leave huge tips for waitresses. You talked to your Heavenly Father freely and openly because you wanted to become intimately acquainted with Him. You read your Bible every spare minute. You didn't care that you weren't perfect. You were simply thankful to be saved. Not complicated at all.

Then you heard 3,456 sermons on how to lead a more godly life, and you read 271 books on how to be a better Christian. You became so confused and rule-oriented that you lost the joy of your salvation. You condemned yourself for not being further along in your walk with Jesus. Because you were ashamed that you weren't perfect, you slacked off on talking to the Lord and reading His Word. All of a sudden, Christianity had become complicated.

Have we tried too hard? Do we want our relationship with God to be like our entertainment: we control it at the flip of a button? We have somehow left the grace of God out of the picture. His grace filled us with joy and love in the beginning of our walk with Him. Because we had never experienced this ecstatic feeling of freedom before, we floated along on His goodness. And, He carried us. We didn't have to try. We simply trusted. Joyous, uncomplicated trust.

Let's go back there, friend. Let's quit trying to control every detail of our lives. Jesus has been here all the time we were struggling on our own, just waiting to "turn up the volume," and do for us what we could not do for ourselves. Just hand Him the remote, and you'll find your life much simpler.

Two Scoops & a Sprinkle

❖ When we try too hard to control our lives, we turn into human doings instead of human beings. Focusing on our own efforts at perfection leads to pride.

❖ Trust requires a certain amount of unanswered questions. We need to be okay with saying, "I don't know, but I don't need to know. I trust you, Lord, because I know you love me."

❖ When you lose something, do you ask God to help you find it? It will save a lot of frustration and wasted time to ask the minute you realize it's missing. The Lord cares about every little thing, even remotes.

The Pact

"Let's make a pact," suggested Kev on one of our frequent walks up a country lane bordered with cornfields, where we talk about everything and nothing.

"What kind of pact did you have in mind?" I cautiously asked. A pact where we agree to not eat desserts on Tuesdays or not complain between 5 and 7 o'clock, I can handle. But don't ask me to quit overreacting, keep my house sparkling clean, or turn my back on a dark chocolate.

"Let's agree that we'll always handle challenges in a mature manner," he said. He managed it with a straight face, too.

I tried to keep it in solitary confinement in my belly, but the laughter escaped, defying me.

"Kevin, we have not handled things in a mature manner for the last thirty-plus years. What makes you believe we can start now?" I don't think my sarcastic attitude hurt him, because he agreed with me. In fact, we stood in the road hee-hawing like two preschoolers who'd discovered their dad's underwear drawer.

Please don't let me mislead you. We are not inept. We raised two responsible adults, have experienced success in our jobs, and most days we keep our sanity in this crazy world. But we've also handled a few situations in embarrassingly immature ways.

As a young wife and mother, I lost my temper and slammed down the lid of my favorite bright green, apple-shaped cookie jar. It was broken beyond repair. The only balm in my sorrow was that there had been no cookies inside.

Another time, Kevin asked me to navigate him to a new friend's house in Los Angeles, and becoming impatient, he grabbed the map from my hand. I should say, he *tried* to grab it. I was so furious with him for implying I didn't know how to read a map, I refused to let go. Two adults, one a preacher and the other a Christian schoolteacher, wrestling with a map. Aha.

My favorite fight occurred on a Sunday evening. We were enjoying the song service as we harmonized to "Leaning on the Everlasting Arms." Kev can harmonize with bullfrogs or bluebirds; he has an excellent ear for chords. But, when he adds his own notes and does doo-wops in my ear, I become as hot as a waffle iron on a Saturday morning.

"Will you please quit singing in my ear?" I whispered, trying not to distract those around us. Kevin grinned like he was five and had just caught his first fish, ignoring my request. On the next song, he continued his musical torture by making up stupid words to the hymn's tune. That's when I lost it.

Whap! Slap! Bap! on his upper arm. "Stop it right *now*," I muttered through gritted teeth. Not even registering the sting of my wimpy attempts at slaps, Kevin laughed aloud, and the older couple behind us couldn't have been more delighted. To witness the preacher's wife beating on the preacher during Sunday evening service was a rare treat, indeed.

What could the Lord be teaching me through these moments of foolishness? Perhaps that the Christian life is a process. God doesn't host an overnight fix-me-up party where I walk through the door with problems, fears, and faults; and once I receive Jesus I quit doing idiotic things and hurting others, including myself.

Things always take longer than you like. Especially the road to spiritual maturity.

God remains patient, however, when we don't make the progress we think we should. He roots and cheers on the sidelines for every little step we make toward Him. All He asks is that we stay in the race.

Although we won't be making any "Maturity From Now On" pacts, the fact that we keep learning and growing even a little bit makes our Father very, very happy. And that's something to laugh about, right in the middle of the road.

Two Scoops & a Sprinkle

❖ Laughing at our foibles and faults is a healthier way to deal with them than condemning each other or ourselves.

❖ God doesn't expect overnight success in our walk with Him. We shouldn't either.

❖ When you are discouraged, thinking you've not progressed a bit since you first became a Christian, ask someone objective to share the growth they've seen in you. Then you do the same favor for her, encouraging each other in your journey to spiritual growth.

The Biggest Trophy

"'Worthy is the Lamb, who was slain, to receive power and wealth and wisdom and strength and honor and glory and praise!'"
(Revelation 5:12 NIV).

Everyone loves trophies. Enterprising award companies make them for anything from the sorest loser (a tantrum-throwing baby) to the ugliest outfit. You can even get one for staying married a long time.

Kevin and I once sang for some friends' fiftieth wedding anniversary. Although never mean or ornery, the husband was what you might call "high-maintenance." The wife was sweet as blueberry pie and never became annoyed by his shenanigans. We wondered how she'd managed to remain unflappable for five decades with Mr. Personality Plus.

They couldn't afford a trip to Hawaii or even New York.

Would a simple party hosted by their kids in the church's fellowship hall prove reward enough for Mrs. Serene Saint?

After a tasty meal, their oldest son called them to the front of the room, which sparkled with gold and white streamers. He draped his arm around his dad's shoulder.

"Dad, we are so proud of you for staying married to Mom all these years. In this society, that's a huge accomplishment. So, we'd like to present you with this token of our admiration." His two sisters joined him to hand their dad a gleaming ten-inch-high trophy. You could spot the dad's grin from the corner gas station.

What a lovely gesture, I thought. *I hope our kids host a party for us when we've been married fifty years. The trophy is a thoughtful touch.* I gulped back tears of joy. Maybe he wasn't such a bad guy after all, if his kids thought so highly of him. Perhaps we'd blown his loud personality out of proportion.

Then, it was the wife's turn. Her eldest son repeated the same heartfelt speech. Tears shone in his mom's eyes. She nodded her thanks as her cheeks flushed pink, trying not to let her self-consciousness show. When the son walked off, saying, "Stay right here, Mom," the room filled with tension. Why did he leave his mother standing there, in front of ninety-five guests?

Returning a few seconds later, he beamed as he presented his mom with an enormous trophy, two-thirds her height. She'd have to haul it home in the back of their pickup. And, the husband laughed the loudest, knowing his forbearing wife had earned every inch of her huge award.

Someday very soon—possibly before you finish reading this—Jesus Christ will return to Earth. Every person who belongs to Him will rocket through the atmosphere to their eternal home, where Jesus will show us each to the door of our custom-made mansion, built by His own hands (John 14).

Before the housewarming parties, however, God will host a fabulous feast in His Son's honor, the Marriage Supper of the Lamb. Can you imagine the awe and excitement that will fill the royal banquet room? We will be in the presence of the King of Creation, the Eternal One, and the Author of Life. Even I will be speechless.

To begin the celebration, the Father will step down from His throne and walk to the front of the hall, where Jesus stands. Holding a mountainous, splendidly wrapped box in His arms, He will ask Jesus to unwrap it, so all can share in His joy. The Father will tell Jesus how proud He is of Him, for being willing to become a man and lay down His life to buy us back from Satan's dominion. Everyone will hold his or her breath as Jesus tears open the glittering wrapping, and it falls to the golden floor.

No one will be surprised when He pulls out the largest trophy ever created. In fact, it will be the only trophy the Father gives. For Jesus alone is worthy of this vast honor: an award from Almighty God.

Two Scoops & a Sprinkle

❖ No one is easy to live with. Ask the Lord for creative ideas to manage frustration over minor annoyances. He wants to help you live in peace, and He has all the answers you need.

❖ In modern society, marriage is not as respected as it once was. Yet God has never changed His mind about the sacredness of this reflection of His love for His bride, the Church. He's always proud of two people who stay married many years.

❖ Although we enjoy the trophies of others, we'll gladly lay them all at Jesus' feet when we meet His Majesty face to face.

I'm Behind You

*"Beloved, you do faithfully whatever you do for the brethren
and for strangers, who have borne witness
of your love before the church"*
(3 John 1:5, 6a, NKJV).

Before Kev and I were married, I worked a short time as a
waitress. I disliked the torture of being on my feet for hours, and
the tacky uniform, complete with a bright orange vinyl apron.
But I learned a useful secret that has saved me dozens of trips to
the medicine chest or the emergency room. It's a phrase every
waiter and waitress learns their first day on the job: "I'm behind
you."

No one wants to turn around and cannon into a tray brimming
with hot coffee, Denver omelets, and oatmeal with raisins.
Fifteen Cub Scouts and their troop leader get impatient when
you have to re-scoop their ice cream because you dropped the

51

original bowls on the floor after forgetting to say "I'm behind you" to the busboy. And your manager with the steaming bowl of vegetable soup may like you better if you remember to say "I'm behind you" as she sails through the break room door. It's wise to let people know of a potential mess, so you both can avoid it.

Tonight, Kevin was getting a pizza out of the oven. I walked behind him, carrying our salad bowls which burst with lovely raw vegetables. Although thirty-plus years have passed since I served food professionally, I still said, "I'm behind you." When those three words hit the air, they gripped my heart in a new way. I was not simply telling Kev to "watch out." I was helping him succeed at his task of the moment. I was supporting and protecting him. We all need this kind of help.

Are you struggling to make ends meet on a stingy budget? If I slip a ten in your pocket, I'm behind you.

Do you doubt if your marriage can last one more night, or one more fight? If I listen and pray for strength for you, I'm behind you.

Are you worried you'll never find a job after you got laid off at age fifty? If I spend hours networking for you and cheering you on, I'm behind you.

Is your kid making choices that break your heart? If I hug you and say, "Don't give up," I'm behind you.

Are you afraid of what the doctor might find on the next test? If I pray for your healing and tell you "I love you," I'm behind you.

Do you wonder where your dream got lost? If I encourage you to keep hoping, I'm behind you.

Rebuking and finding fault rarely motivate anyone to succeed. Most of us avoid critical, sour individuals. But we love to be near people who bring out the best in us, helping us believe in ourselves and our dreams. We achieve goals we thought impossible by having just one or two caring friends say, "I'm behind you."

You can be that friend to someone today. Instead of turning your back on a need or mocking a dream, be wise enough to say "I'm behind you. Let me help you succeed."

For your fellow servers, it will make the difference between messes to clean up or miracles to celebrate.

Two Scoops & a Sprinkle

❖ Supporting someone when she needs cheering up can be as small as a hug or as large as prayer for a miracle. Most people don't need fancy. They only want to know someone is on their side.

❖ When you say "I'm behind you" by helping another accomplish their dreams, you're planting seeds for the fulfillment of your own dreams.

❖ The Lord never runs out of ways to tell us "I'm behind you." If you're feeling alone, it's okay to ask Him for some reassurance. He may surprise you by the creative ways He chooses to encourage you.

Cow Chip Classic

*" 'These things I have spoken to you, so that in Me you may
have peace. In the world you have tribulation, but take
courage; I have overcome the world' "*
(John 16:33 NASB).

When I shook Jeremy's hand during greeting time in church, I
glanced down at his bright red shirt and read *Cow Chip Classic,
2006.* Rather than stewing over the message on his shirt, I was
thrilled he chose to spend his Sunday morning worshiping God.
Besides, it gave me an opportunity to find out what a Cow Chip
Classic is.

As a city transplant, I envisioned overall-clad people throwing
cow chips in a pasture like discuses at a track meet. The chipper
who threw the farthest got a prize, like a new milking stool or a
branding iron. "Is that how it worked?" I asked Jeremy.

"No," he said, smiling politely. "We just raced across the
field, dodging cow chips along the way."

I wrinkled my nose as my imagination raced across the patty-laden field with all the marathoners. Although I was almost afraid to know, I asked anyway, "Did you step in any?"

His smile grew into a grin. "A few."

I grinned back, but couldn't help thinking, *Why would anyone want to run through a field of cow chips? That's way too much like real life.*

A few days on this earth are sunny and bright. The chickadees sing sweetly in the peach trees, the smell of new-mown hay tickles your nose as you drive down the highway, and the price of gas is lower than last week. No cow chips scattered in your field. But some days are like this. . . .

It's raining *again*, all the chickadees in the peach trees are either pouting or scrapping with each other, the only smell as you drive down the highway is the dead skunk you just ran over, and gas prices are up *again*. Your pasture is full of those darn cow chips. You're bound to step in a few.

Life stinks sometimes. No matter how deftly you dodge between the cow chips, you cannot avoid them all. Some even seem to jump out of the grass and land smack in front of you. By the time you reach the end—or even the middle—of the field, you're a dirty mess. And your shoes need to go into the dumpster.

Jesus predicted as much when He told His followers, "In the world you will have tribulation (John 16:33)." To His credit, He didn't stop there, or we may have said, "Thanks a lot, Lord. Tell me something I don't already know." His next words add a fragrant scent to our smelly situations: "But be of good cheer. I have overcome the world." The *Amplified Bible* version says, "I have deprived it of power to harm you."

Wow.

No matter how many times you've tripped or fallen in those cow pies, no matter how stinky your life has become, Jesus offers you His hope. If you trust in His amazing promises, all the cow chips in the world cannot permanently harm you. He has deprived them of their power to ruin you. He has overcome them on your behalf.

My word for that kind of love? Classic.

Two Scoops & a Sprinkle

❖ When tempted to despair and beg Jesus to return *today* to take me home to Heaven, I remember all the suffering He endured to give me a place in His family. Somehow, this exercise lends perspective to my viewpoint.

❖ Helping someone who's in a stinkier situation than mine is another way I overcome self-pity. I don't have to look long or far to find someone like that.

❖ On occasion, the cow chips in my field were caused by my own foolishness or sin. When that's the case, I need to admit my wrong and repent. Then I humbly ask the Lord for His mercy, the perfect cleanup for my messes.

Keepers

"My sheep hear my voice, and I know them, and they follow Me; and I give eternal life to them, and they will never perish; and no one will snatch them out of my hand"
(John 10:27-28 NASB).

While chatting with Grandma, three-year-old Esther's reasoning made perfect sense: "Mommy says we can have a pet as soon as baby-Ron is old enough to help me take care of it. I decided I want a kitty instead of a puppy, because kitties cover up their poo-poos!"

Shortly after this astute observation, we let the kids get their first cat, and we've not stopped collecting them since. In fact, I've owned cats—oops—they've owned me—since I was six.

Because he was pure black, I named my first cat Beebee. He'd called us his family only two years when he came up missing. We hollered and hunted for two days. By the time we found him under a bush, he was severely dehydrated and weak, his back leg mangled from a fight.

The vet thought it best to put him to sleep. "Beebee's leg needs to be amputated," he explained, looking down on my tear-drenched freckles. "He won't be able to climb trees or defend himself with only three legs."

I sobbed all the way home after telling Beebee good-bye, but my single mom could not afford a second opinion.

Years later, I read accounts of both cats and dogs that had survived a limb amputation and lived full lives with only three limbs. If only we had known.

I don't think of Beebee too often, other than to wish I'd had enough spunk to say, "Let's try to save him. Let's not throw him away, just because he isn't perfect. We'll love him all the more."

Is this our attitude with people, relationships, churches, and jobs? Or does our desire for perfection cause us to toss aside what could prove useful, given a little loving help?

I wonder how many disciples Jesus would have kept if He'd required perfection, or at least the image of it.

Peter would have been the first one Jesus booted out. He made a habit of talking first, then afterward trying to douse the flames. When Jesus told His followers that He was going to suffer crucifixion, Peter had the audacity to argue, "Oh no, Lord, this will never be!" That stupid comment prompted Jesus to box him verbally, saying, "Get behind me, Satan!"

Then, the pragmatic Thomas. Brokenhearted over Jesus' death, he refused to believe his friends' witness regarding the resurrection. He stubbornly declared, "My faith can only be based on what I see." Jesus corrected this faithless thinking. He stated that we who believe in Him without seeing are more blessed than the prideful, proof-requiring Thomas.

None of the disciples made perfect followers. Nor do we. But Jesus refused to give up on them, in spite of their immaturity, foolishness, or bad habits. Just as He refuses to give up on you or me.

Let's embrace hope in Jesus' willingness to love, nurture, and heal us, no matter where we find ourselves on our journey with Him. Missing leg, big mouth, failed faith, or broken heart—His love makes up for our lack.

In this world of "throw away" everything, Jesus calls all of us keepers.

Two Scoops & a Sprinkle

❖ Not only are we sometimes tempted to discard others who seem broken beyond repair, but we also can feel like giving up on ourselves. When this emotion threatens to steal our peace, Jesus is nearby. Full of mercy and understanding, He never gives up on us.

❖ Only one Person is perfect, but He's not a perfectionist. Wanting to grow in the Lord is a noble goal; perfectionism involves unrealistic expectations. If you are stuck in the mire of perfectionism, open your heart to receive God's grace. Now, relax and enjoy yourself, just as you are.

❖ Just as Jesus worked through fallible men to turn the world upside down, He will work through us to accomplish His purposes today.

God's Logic

"'For my thoughts are not your thoughts, neither are your ways my ways,' declares the Lord. 'As the heavens are higher than the earth, so are my ways higher than your ways and my thoughts than your thoughts'"
(Isaiah 55:8-9 NIV).

"Why did you wave to that car?" asked Kevin as we were returning home from a trip to town.

"I always wave at large, maroon cars, in case it's Donna Bell."

"Honey, that *man* did not look anything like Donna Bell."

"I know that now, but by the time I get close enough to see the person's face, it's too late to wave, and I don't want Donna to think I'm ignoring her," I argued. "I also wave at bright red vans, just in case it's Tammy Bennett or the Robertsons."

He grinned in my direction and said, "You are a character. But I will never understand your logic."

"That makes two of us," I said.

Have you noticed that everyone has a different sort of logic? For instance, where do you put your silverware? Nearest the table, so when you or your child is setting it, it's most convenient? Or close to the sink, so when you dry dishes, you can easily fling the forks into the drawer? Some people may not use silverware at all, preferring to eat only finger foods, thus saving money on washing forks and spoons.

Because it helps me dress faster, I have my clothes arranged in my closet by color. My husband arranges his by garments: the shirts in one place, the pants in another. His brain best understands this method, even though it would slow me down. But that's okay. I don't have to wear his clothes.

Some people like to pray first thing in the morning when they're fresh, others at night, so they can be thinking of God as they drop off to sleep.

No two people think exactly alike when it comes to how to do things. Which is a good thing. It makes the world much more interesting.

Have you also noticed God's logic?

He says, "If you are depressed, sing and thank Me. Meditate on my goodness to recover your joy." Really? I would have reached for the chocolate, e-mailed a friend so that I could vent my pain, or invited myself to a pity party.

He says, "If someone wrongs you, bless them and pray for them." Hmm. My way would have been to check them off my Christmas card list, pretending I'd never met them, so I didn't have to deal with the hurt.

He says, "If you want to be great in my kingdom, be the servant of all." You mean, don't host my own parade? Don't criticize others to make myself look better?

He says, "To gain eternal life, deny your flesh and follow me." Oh. Then I can't do salvation on my own terms, by trying to be righteous and doing, doing, doing what to me looks "good"? I have to give up my own way and follow you, Lord?

Nearly everything we would naturally do to manage people and situations, God manages in the opposite way. And, how about that—His methods work. It never fails when we do things God's ways instead of our own.

When we decide to trade our logic for His, reading His Book to find out His plans, we end up thinking His thoughts. We have some remarkable, supernatural results.

Our unpredictable reasoning for His perfect logic—not a bad trade.

Two Scoops & a Sprinkle

❖ We can question God's logic, but His ways always work. Seems logical to me that we'd save time and frustration if we agree and do it His way from the outset.

❖ The Lord usually puts people together as friends or spouses who have opposite styles of logic. I believe He does this on purpose to entertain Himself. He needs a good laugh as often as the rest of us.

❖ When we combine our various types of logic and collaborate rather than trying to force others to see it our way, God is glorified, and our lives run smoother.

Do What You Can

"Let us consider how to stimulate one another to love and good deeds"
(Hebrews 10:24 NASB).

When asked to speak for the Homemakers' Club at a Christian nursing home, I was stumped. I emerged from the womb yakking, singing, and trying to motivate others (some call it bossing). Still, what could I say to inspire women twice my age, and probably ten times my spiritual stature?

I went to the One with all the answers.

"Lord, I could use your help. Many of these ladies are in wheelchairs. Some of them are sick. Most will never leave the nursing home. What can I share with them to add some meaning to their lives?"

The idea came swiftly, with surprising results.

"There are people all around you who need your unique talents and abilities," I chirped to the dozen ladies gracing the room with their brightly flowered dresses. Although they listened kindly, I detected a shadow of doubt in their eyes. Perhaps I'd missed God's voice and brought the wrong message. They must have thought me blind or naive, not to notice their hands twisted with arthritis and their useless legs in the wheelchair footrests.

Nevertheless, I forged ahead. This was the message I believed God had put on my heart. I had to trust His voice rather than my eyes.

"While you may not be able to do everything you once did, the Lord can use you to touch many lives. God doesn't require a brilliant mind or a perfect body for you to make a positive difference in the world. What He's searching for is a willing heart. He just wants you to do what you can."

To jumpstart the ladies' discovery of unique ways to touch others' lives, I passed around a jar filled with colorful slips of paper. On each one, I had written a simple idea. Every club member chose two papers and read the ideas aloud. Here are a few examples:

- *Give a smile to someone who lost his or hers.*
- *Hug a lonely neck or pat a sagging shoulder.*
- *Say "thank you" to a nurse or cook.*
- *Write a note to a friend, just to say, "I'm thinking of you."*
- *«Pray for a serviceman or woman who is far from home and family.*
- *Read a story to a sightless friend.*

- *Share a joke with someone who needs to laugh.*
- *Give a genuine compliment to a person you admire.*
- *Sing a happy song or hymn to a discouraged soul.*
- *Compose a silly poem to brighten someone's day.*

The lady who picked "compose a silly poem" rushed back to her room and returned with a bright blue notebook. She was a poet, and had recently written a ridiculous one that she read on the spot. Our laughter danced to the ceiling.

Others chattered with each other, planning who would receive their blessings. God had broken through the doubt long tucked away in their hearts. He'd inspired these seasoned saints to do what they could, right where they were, to touch lives. I felt humbled that I'd heard from Him, and joyful that He'd used me. It was a divine moment.

Several days later, I recalled the evening. A yummy delight filled my soul. "Thank you, Father, for your splendid idea! You always go above and beyond what I ask or dream. You are so amazing."

A familiar Voice stole into my heart, soft and steady: "What made you think I meant that idea for those ladies alone?"

Two Scoops & a Sprinkle

❖ God enjoys taking ordinary people and changing the world with them. No one sits on the bench in His team.

❖ Visiting a nursing home can cause our hearts to overflow with gratitude for all we have and can do.

❖ Older saints may not have physical strength, but they often overflow with divine wisdom. We do ourselves a favor when we seek their godly counsel.

From Hair to Eternity

"Since God assured us, 'I'll never let you down, never walk off
and leave you,' we can boldly quote,
'God is ready to help; I'm fearless no matter what.
Who or what can get to me?'"
(Hebrews 13:5 The Message).

As I fixed my hair for work one morning, I whined to Kevin about how horrible it looked.

He smiled and said, "Yeah, it does look pretty bad."

To tell you I came unglued would be to say the Pacific Ocean is larger than a puddle. Dropping my pick and my jaw into the sink, I looked at him in disbelief and feminine fury.

My voice rose to the cobwebs in the bathroom corners and through the roof. "Kev—never, never, never tell a woman her hair looks bad. That is something you should never, ever do, ever. As in, *never!*" My high school voice teacher from decades ago would have been proud of those effortless high notes.

His brows wrinkled in confusion. "But we just had this long conversation about being agreeable," he said.

"There are certain rules that apply to certain situations, but not all." My heart pounded. "By agreeing that my hair looks terrible, you're jumping into the ring with me. You can say, 'I'm sorry you feel that way; I think it looks fine,' or, 'Do you need some money to get it fixed today, honey?' But to say, 'Yes, you're right,' when a woman just told you her hair is a shame to the female gender is an unforgivable sin in the world of matrimony. Hair is a sacred topic for women, especially between the ages of five and ninety."

Afterwards, I had a good laugh at my over-the-top reaction, but I still meant every word I'd said. Especially the word *never.*

God takes that word *never* seriously too. He says in Hebrews 13:5 (*NKJV*), "I will never leave you nor forsake you."

Are you thinking, "Yeah, right. Then where was God when my daddy left, my sister was born deformed, my wife walked out, my child (parent, friend) died?"

Although you may not have been aware of Him, God was right there beside you. He was keeping you sane, enabling you to survive those terrible ordeals, and bringing people across your path to help and heal you. He never once turned His back on you or stopped caring for you. If He had, you wouldn't be here reading these words.

God does not prevent evil, like a huge wizard pulling levers to compel mankind to behave as He pleases. He refuses to force people to act against their wills. Because of that freedom to choose, innocent people suffer.

But if we ask and allow Him to, the Lord will ensure that somehow, some way, good crops spring up in the soil of sorrow and pain. He will give us beauty for ashes and joy for tears. He is more than willing to redeem the most horrible circumstances of our lives to make us into stronger, kinder, richer people as a result.

I can't fix you. I can't even fix me. But I know Someone who can. He has promised never to leave us. From bad hair days to seasons of sorrow and destruction, we can depend on God's promise to hold us in His heart and hands.

From hair to eternity.

Two Scoops & a Sprinkle

❖ As long as we blame the Lord for the pain in our lives, we won't trust His love enough to turn to Him for help.

❖ There's a difference between being agreeable and being too honest, to the point of inflicting unnecessary hurt on others.

❖ One of God's most amazing qualities is His ability to take horrible situations and redeem them for good in our lives.

Adventures in Fasting

"'Is this not the fast which I choose, to loosen the bonds of wickedness, to undo the bands of the yoke, and to let the oppressed go free and to break every yoke?'"
(Isaiah 58:6 NASB).

I wonder if I should fast, I thought. *She sounded serious in her e-mail.*

My friend Allison's doctor had scheduled her for an MRI. This was a routine checkup following a brain operation the previous year, and she was nervous. I had been praying, but an extra *oomph* seemed in order. That's when I got the idea to fast.

I realize that fasting isn't a method for manipulating God. It's more a way to humble yourself, so you can hear His voice. It's getting serious about being in the center of His will. And nothing spells serious like going without food.

My problem is, I become Miss Cranky Pants when I miss a meal. This isn't good if you work with the public, serve in ministry, and write a newspaper column called "God is Bigger."

As I pondered my dilemma, I noticed the book we were studying in Sunday school: *Me and My Big Mouth*. I flipped it over to read the chapter headings on the back. One of them grabbed me by the throat: *Fasting Includes Your Mouth*. Oh dear.

More research led me to Isaiah 58, where God rebukes the Israelites for fasting food but continuing to sin with their speech and wicked attitudes. The word that poked my conscience was in verse 9, where God says, "Remove the pointing of the finger and speaking wickedness."

I'll fast complaining, I thought. *Every time I'm tempted to grumble or be negative, I'll pray for Allison instead.* I was so proud of my bright idea, I began immediately.

While getting ready for work, the thought presented itself to criticize my hair. *What good is it to have naturally curly hair if the curls don't go the direction I want?* Oops! Fasting complaining; I almost forgot. "Lord, help Allison to not be scared today during her MRI. Let her feel your presence." While rushing to check e-mails before leaving the house, I was tempted to grump about my overflowing inbox: *If Merry Mug Shots didn't notify me every time someone sneezed, I could manage these e-mails better.* Oops! Fasting whining. Pray instead. "Father, speak to Allison during her test today, please. Help her believe your love for her."

All morning I fought with griping gremlins and disparaging demons. By the time I looked at the clock and realized Allison's test was over, I felt like I'd wrestled a grizzly with my bare hands. And I wasn't sure who'd won.

I'd mistakenly thought taming my tongue would be easier than going without candy or donuts. I was wrong. The habit of negative words was stronger than my appetite for food.

Over the next few days, the Lord showed me my need to control not just what went into my mouth but also what came out of it. Leading me to Scriptures about the tongue, and revealing to me how my words affected the moods of those around me, were gifts from Him.

Was I grateful to the Holy Spirit for loving me enough to show me where I'm failing? *Yes.*

Was it easy to discover how out of control my mouth had become? *No.*

Because my calling is to communicate God's grace, self-control over my tongue remains my greatest challenge. Every day I'm tempted to gripe, find the potholes instead of the pavement, and point out nits and zits. Realizing this character flaw and my need for constant restraint has humbled me. And that's a good thing.

Another good thing that resulted from my realization of the need to be more positive? Allison got a ton of prayer, and splendid test results.

Two Scoops & a Sprinkle

❖ Don't feel less than spiritual if you can't manage a food fast. Try a grumbling- or negative-attitude fast. Substitute praise and prayer in their place and see how God works.

❖ Some believers have found it effective to fast television or the Internet for a time, using the extra minutes or hours gained to pray.

❖ When the Holy Spirit reveals a gap in our souls, His purpose is to heal us and fill us with more of Jesus' nature. He never convicts to condemn. He shines a holy light to bring us out of darkness and bless others with His love.

I Believe in Blabbing

"Watch the way you talk. Let nothing foul or dirty come out of your mouth. Say only what helps, each word a gift"
(Ephesians 4:29 The Message).

"Don't be a blabbermouth," Mom always told me. But I discovered Mom wasn't right every time. It can be helpful to blab.

I'll bet Phillip Collier, one of the deacons in our church, agrees with me.

As I shook Phillip's hand one Sunday after church, the light from a vestibule window caught a flash somewhere near the floor. I gazed down at a pair of black Oxfords, gleaming like a showroom car.

I thought, *I wonder what time he sets his alarm every Sunday to make his shoes shine like that.* I blinked a few times and pointed (another bad habit Mom had forbidden). "Your shoes remind me of Jesus, Phillip."

79

He shook his head, confusion clouding his eyes. "My shoes? Why?"

"There's a verse in Isaiah that says, 'How lovely on the mountains are the feet of those who bring good news.' When I see those dazzling shoes as you pass the communion tray each Sunday, I remember the good news of Jesus, how He came to Earth to show us God's love. Don't laugh, but your shoes minister His grace to me."

To his credit, Phillip didn't laugh. The clouded look cleared as he said, "Back when I was in Army boot camp, our commanding officer told us, 'Shoes are the first thing people notice when you walk up, and the last thing they see when you leave. They are both your first and last impression.' That comment stayed with me. I've always tried to keep my shoes looking nice since then."

"They're nice all right," I answered. "I could comb my hair in their reflection if I needed to." He walked to his car, still shaking his head. As he slipped into the seat, I caught a hint of a smile inching its way up his face.

Which makes me glad I blabbed to Phillip.

If I'd kept my thoughts to myself, he'd never have known what a blessing his highly polished shoes gave me, and I'd never have seen that beatific smile on his face, which I hope outshone the shoes by the time he reached home. You see? We're both richer people because I blabbed.

Most individuals think blabbing only serves for telling the offenses or secrets of others. But I love to blab about the good things I see, to brighten someone's day. I blab to my assistant about her brilliant ideas for solving a problem. I blab to my husband about his outstanding sermons and creative songs. I blab to the waitress on her excellent service. The opportunities for blabbing are limitless.

Just make sure when you blab, it's for the right reason: to plant seeds of encouragement in another's life. Because you never know when you might need a harvest of hopeful words for yourself one day.

I'm sorry, Mom. This is one time I'm going to disregard your instructions in order to follow God's. He told me to build others up and let my words give them grace (Ephesians 4:29). I'd say my kind of blabbing fits that description better than a pair of custom-made Oxfords on a deacon.

Two Scoops & a Sprinkle

❖ Is there someone in your life you've silently admired? Contact them this week and blab to them why you think they're terrific. Don't wait until they move away or pass away to encourage them.

❖ A backdoor approach to blabbing is to tell someone what compliments others have given them behind their backs. This creates good feelings between people who might never give or hear a compliment face to face.

❖ How do you receive it when someone blabs to you about your fine qualities? Graciousness is a sign of humility and love.

Honest to God

"In the same way, the Spirit helps us in our weakness. We do not know what we ought to pray for, but the Spirit himself intercedes for us with groans that words cannot express" **(Romans 8:26 NIV).**

We caught our daughter, Esther, in her first lie at the venerable age of three. When I confronted her with, "Is that the truth?" she innocently replied, "It's *my* truth!"

Everyone applauds and respects honesty in a person. Honesty inspires us to emulate people like George Washington and Abraham Lincoln. According to one survey, people expect honesty in a close relationship above every other virtue. When it comes to our relationship with God, however, we usually are anything but honest.

The Bible tells us God knew us before we were even born. He knew every word out of our mouths, every thought and intention of our hearts. Yet how often do we come in prayer or worship and say the things we think He wants to hear, rather than what really troubles our minds and fills our hearts?

We say, "It's okay that I have not found a job yet, Lord, even though I've been unemployed for sixteen months. I know you have a plan, and I will trust you to the end."

We think, *What is up with this, Lord? Are you punishing me for some past sin? I don't understand why this is taking so long. I need some answers, now.*

We say, "There is a reason for everything that happens. You are in control, God."

We feel: *Lord, this is not fair! I have been serving you with my whole heart, yet people are criticizing me right and left. Can't you do something to vindicate me, and shut their mouths?*

We say, "I know it's a sin to worry, so I trust you with my children's lives, Lord. I cast the care of them on you."

We want to say, *Oh God, this should not be happening! Do something before they destroy themselves and me along with them! I don't know how much more of this I can endure!*

God is never shocked by anything we say, do, or think. We can't take Him by surprise or ruin His day by our frankness and honesty. He wants us to be completely open with Him, so He can heal us where we hurt and fix the broken places in our lives. Without candor, we can never achieve the intimate relationship with Him that we need and want.

In the Bible, all of God's closest friends shared a brutal frankness with Him. Abraham argued with the Lord over destroying Sodom and Gomorrah. As Jacob wrestled with God he said, "I'll not let you go until you bless me." Moses told Him to find someone else to lead the Israelites out of Egypt. David accused Him of not keeping His word—can you imagine the nerve? Even Jesus wailed, "Why have you forsaken me?" as He hung dying. God did not rebuke one of these for their raw, human attitudes.

Do we cheat ourselves of precious times of fellowship and life-changing insights by sugarcoating our prayers and telling God only what we think He enjoys hearing? God wants to be your best friend. But He can't give you the answers you need if you are hiding behind false feelings and worthless words. You have to be real to get healed. You have to be honest to God.

Two Scoops & a Sprinkle

❖ Nothing surprises God. Why not be forthright with Him? Who else has the heart to love you as you are and the power to help you improve?

❖ Even if we are angry or disappointed with God, it won't hurt His feelings when we tell Him so. And it may help us develop a more open relationship with Him to share the anguish of our soul as well as the joy.

❖ Don't stop with telling the Lord your junk. Give Him the opportunity to show you the way out of it by sitting quietly and listening for His insights. Keep your Bible nearby—He speaks most often through its wisdom.

Ice Cream Snatcher

"He who did not spare his own Son, but gave him up for us all—how will he not also, along with him, graciously give us all things?"
(Romans 8:32 NIV).

Can you believe our gorgeous, talented granddaughter's parents rarely allow her to eat ice cream or other sweets? How cruel is that?

We decided to make up for this parental meanness when Jenessa was a year and a half old by taking her to an ice cream shop near her home in Broken Arrow, Oklahoma. Although we would not buy her a cone of her own, we would let her have as much of ours as her little heart desired.

Wasn't that part of our job as Gramma and Grampa? "We spanked the kids; we spoil the grandkids" is our motto. So, down we rolled to Braum's, and ordered our chocolate chunky doodle and peach cobbler delight.

Jenessa behaved like a cherub for the first ten minutes in her bright yellow booster chair, taking licks as we offered them. The cones were so huge she could not have handled one on her own, anyway. I think it gratified us to know we were indulging her in something Mom and Dad had forbidden. To be honest, we were probably on some kind of middle-aged power trip.

Unexpectedly, this angelic child lost her halo. When Grampa had eaten his cone down to a manageable size for her chubby little paw, she ripped it right out of his hand and stuffed it into her mouth.

Before we were done laughing, before we could say, "Hey, you!" she had unashamedly devoured it, with only a fudgy drip on her chin as evidence.

Don't be further shocked, but we didn't even get mad. We took it as a compliment that this beloved baby would consider our ice cream hers. After all, wasn't our entire goal to share what we had with her? We felt pleased that she was comfortable enough with us to—literally—take our possessions from our hands.

Jenessa's boldness characterizes what God longs to see in all His children's hearts. When He says, "Here, I want to share with you," we need to be comfortable enough with Him to reach out and take it.

Where have we found the odd, unbiblical idea that we have to be at a certain level spiritually before we can expect big blessings or huge miracles from God? We have erroneously thought we needed to behave angelically before we can come to His throne and ask for large favors. Or we've refused to receive because of some past sin we've never forgiven ourselves for.

There is not a thing we can do to earn God's love, favor, or answers to our prayers, just as Jenessa has done nothing to earn our love and goodness. She was born into our family. That made her fair game for all the love, favor, gifts, and ice cream we could rain on her.

We could live to be 310 and still not be good enough to merit God's kindness and generosity. If we are born again by the blood of Jesus into God's family, that gives us the right to all God has and all He offers. When we reach out to receive the blessings He offers, we need not feel guilty. It delights the Father to give to His children. Let Him have some fun today. Let Him love you by simply reaching out in childlike faith and saying, "Thank you, I'll take it."

Two Scoops & a Sprinkle

❖ Humility is not saying, "Oh no, don't give me anything—I'm not good enough." Humility is knowing who's in charge, and submitting to Him. If He wants to give us blessings, we humble ourselves by receiving them with a thankful heart.

❖ Some things that stand in the way of receiving from the Lord are strife with a brother or sister, worry, negative talk, and worldly pursuits.

❖ If it's easy for us to give but difficult to receive, we may suffer from a need to be in control.

Do You Want a Spanking?

"Beloved, it is a fine and faithful work that you are doing when you give any service to the [Christian] brethren, and [especially when they are] strangers"
(3 John 1:5 Amplified Bible).

When our kids were kids, we traveled to churches and sang on Sunday evenings and vacation times. Kevin and I like to believe that people enjoyed our original music, but I think they were attracted by the children's singing, and their unpredictable antics.

One church that we performed an evening concert for had their restrooms in a separate building from the main auditorium. Before the concert, I headed across the parking lot to the ladies room. I thought Ron was with Kevin, but he'd followed me and waited outside the door while I went in.

It was crowded that night, so I had to stand in line. I hadn't even taken my turn yet when the racket started:

"Mommmyyyy! Are you in there, Mommmy? Can you hurry up, please?"

I didn't want to lose my place in line by opening the door to tell him "hush," so I just counted the specks in the tiles on the floor, pretending to feel sorry for whoever's little blessing was outside hollering. I prayed that the line would speed up or Ron would shut up. Neither did. By the time I was ready to leave, my blood was boiling.

I stomped across the room and flung open the door, shouting into the darkness, "Do you want a spanking?"

An older lady stared back at me with a shocked expression. "No, I don't."

"Oh, I'm so sorry," I said, my cheeks hot. I didn't even try to explain, just rushed out to find my little circus barker turned Houdini. I found him around the corner of the building where he'd conveniently slipped seconds before. As I ushered him across the parking lot, I delivered the Mom's lecture #34: *Unless you are bleeding or the house is on fire, do not interrupt me when I'm going potty. Especially if I'm in a public restroom with fourteen other ladies.*

Although we traveled and sang for more than fifteen years and performed hundreds of concerts, I always wanted our ministry to reach farther afield.

One day I lamented to the Lord how small a difference I felt we were making in His kingdom. I wanted to be Sandi Patti and Michael W. Smith with the Von Trapp Family Singers. Comparison never leads anywhere holy, so the Lord stopped me with His gentle voice in my heart.

"Jeanette, yours is a ministry of encouragement. You may not perform a glamorous program, but your songs give hope. How important is the gift of hope when you're discouraged?"

"Oh, Lord, I'd give my right arm and elbow for a glimmer of hope in those times I'm ready to quit." Then He reminded me of a concert we'd sung a few weeks before.

In the back row had sat a forty-ish man who gazed with unblinking eyes the entire thirty minutes we sang. His face was a rock. I wondered if we were getting through to this brother at all. Still, I sang my heart out for the Master, pouring my voice onto His altar.

At the end of the concert, Mr. Brickface came to me. With tear-filled eyes and cracking voice, he said, "I want to tell you how much your ministry encouraged me. I am bipolar. Your music lifted me to Heaven tonight. Thank you so much for coming to our church and singing."

His words showed me that our ministry, although not worldwide or flashy, was touching lives and helping people find a ray of light for their darkened souls.

We rarely travel and sing these days. But I like to think our music planted some hope in a few hearts along the way. Even if one lady is wondering why a crazy redhead asked if she wanted a spanking outside the ladies' room twenty-some years ago.

Two Scoops & a Sprinkle

- ❖ God isn't impressed with glitz, but a willing, obedient heart. He doesn't require perfection to minister for Him. If He did, no one would qualify.
- ❖ We can't judge whether we're getting through to someone by the look on his or her face. Some people need time to process what the Lord is telling them through a message or song. He works far below the surface to change hearts.
- ❖ Children rarely behave predictably in public settings. Let them be kids. Don't worry too much what other people think.

Honey, Have You Seen My Teeth?

"Rejoice with those who rejoice, and
weep with those who weep"
(Romans 12:15 NKJV).

On a day barely begun, Joanna's son Paul answered the door to a man wearing a conservative black suit.

"Sorry to bother you this early, Paul, but I need to get your dad's teeth so we can start embalming today. We forgot to ask for them last night when we picked up his body."

"Oh, okay," Paul muttered, rubbing sleep from his eyes and scratching his chest through wrinkled pajamas. "Come on in. I'll see if Mom can find them for you."

Before Paul finished talking, Joanna appeared in the living room, tying her robe about her slender waist. "Back so soon, Sam? What did we forget? I always said I'd forget my head if it wasn't glued on." Even on the morning after her husband's death, Joanna's indomitable spirit kept her sense of humor in place.

Paul winced as he looked at her bloodshot eyes. "We forgot Dad's teeth, Mom."

Joanna shuffled to the bathroom, and returned a minute later with a pink D-shaped container.

"Here you go."

"Thanks, Joanna," said Paul, "I promise this is the last time we'll bother you."

That afternoon, as she and Paul got ready to go out to lunch, Joanna called from the bathroom, "Honey, have you seen my teeth?"

"Didn't you have them in when Sam came this morning?"

Joanna's voice creaked like the back door of her old house. "No, I just got out of bed long enough to throw my robe on and fetch him your dad's teeth. . . . Oh, Paul, you don't think?"

"I do think, Mom. Your teeth are in Dad's mouth!"

She was silent for a second, and then threw back her head and laughed. "Well, then, I did get the last word in after all, didn't I?"

Bless the dentist who scurried to make a set of teeth for Joanna in time for the funeral the next day. Although we were grieved over the passing of her husband, the telling of the teeth story added a sweet note to his service.

Kevin tries to include something humorous or lighthearted about the deceased in every funeral he conducts. Even though we take grief seriously, it helps us manage our pain if we can laugh a little through the tears.

People who've been forced to say good-bye to a loved one may be angry at the Lord or the one who died, abandoning them. They are in shock. They feel overwhelmed with extra responsibilities and loneliness. The best kinds of comfort come in the form of little acts of kindness.

Perhaps cooking a meal or having them over to share supper with your family would make them feel less alone. Offering to help balance a checkbook, take them shopping, or just sitting to chat may help fill the gaping void in their hearts. Most of all, hugs, words of love, and prayers are what these hurting souls need at this horrible time.

And possibly, a new set of teeth.

Two Scoops & a Sprinkle

❖ Until Jesus returns and makes all things new, death will be a part of our lives. For the Christian, it means moving from an earthly house to a heavenly one, free from pain and disease.

❖ Funerals and memorial services help those left behind to cope with their loss. It's okay to cry. It hurts to have someone leave you, even though you know it's temporary. It's also okay to laugh about fun times you shared. Laughter heals.

❖ Most people shower the bereaved with attention for a week or two after their loss, and then forget about them. Grief takes more than a week to process. Gestures as simple as a card in the mail or an invitation to go along on a picnic will show these sorrowing ones you still care long after the funeral flowers have wilted.

The Divine No

"For as the heavens are higher than the earth, so are My ways higher than your ways, and My thoughts than your thoughts"
(Isaiah 55:9 NKJV).

As a parent, I flopped at saying "no." Having grown up with an unreasonable stepdad, I preferred the kind and friendly "maybe" or "we'll see," which usually translated to "yes." This penchant for affirmatives explains why the kids came to me for favors fifty times more often than they asked Kevin, because his "maybe" meant "no."

A few times, I surprised myself and embraced a "no" with fervor. Once was when Ron wanted to quit school. He had recently celebrated his tenth birthday, and approached me with a proclamation: "Mom, I already know everything, so I don't need to go to school anymore."

"I don't think so, Ron. You know a lot, but you don't know everything. You are not quitting school."

Stubborn tears clouded his eyes. "I do, Mom. *I know everything!*" I would have laughed if he weren't so serious. I softened my voice in mercy, but remained firm. "Nevertheless, Ron, you are staying in school."

That event took place over twenty years ago. Two Bachelor of Arts degrees now hang on Ron's wall from the university where he made the dean's list several times. I hope he's thankful I stuck to my "no."

When Esther was a teenager wanting to wear tight jeans, watch R-rated movies, and date before she was ready, we squared our shoulders, lifted our chins, and remained impervious to her cries of, "Everyone else . . ." That was more than two decades ago. I'm convinced her husband is relieved we told her "no."

How many times God has said no to me, and I thought He was being unreasonable like my stepdad, but later discovered He was steering me away from danger or toward blessings. Like a child, I could not comprehend why God refused to give me what I wanted. With adult perception, I see that His no was the kindest form of love.

God's no in my life meant moving to Paris, Illinois, where Kevin and I pastor the most devoted flock we've had in over thirty years of ministry. We live in a large, lovely house and are part of a warm and caring community.

After we left our last church, I told God dozens of times that I did not want to go back into the ministry. I enjoyed living as an ordinary person with no pressure to carry out anyone's expectations, no pedestal to balance upon, and no pristine role model to fulfill. I didn't want to leave the friendships I had built up over twenty years, or my favorite restaurants and malls.

But God knew better. He knew we'd make supportive new friends, find new cafés, and never miss those crowded malls. He knew that moving us to the Midwest would open doors of ministry that we'd never had in L.A. So He said "no." And we're thankful He did.

At times, it's necessary to say through tears of disappointment and an aching heart, "Lord, I know you love me, and I trust you. If you say no, it must be because saying yes would hurt me."

It's okay to tell God you are disappointed, even angry, at how something has turned out. But then trust His goodness more than you trust your own perspective. He can see over the next hill in our lives. He knows better than we do what roadblocks will keep us from succeeding, and what fruit stands will nourish us along the way.

We grow to believe His love enough to accept the "no's" when they come, and realize that someday we'll thank Him when our name ends up on the dean's list or we find "Mr. Wonderful." Because God's no is divine, He turns it into a yes for us. He's the only Dad who can do that.

Two Scoops & a Sprinkle

❖ Remembering the blessings that have resulted from God's "no's" have helped me accept them, even when I thought I knew best.

❖ Only those who've never grown up won't take no for an answer. Mature Christians have developed a secure belief in God's love and commitment to their highest good.

❖ When I'm not sure of God's will in a matter, I need to work at keeping my emotions out of the equation. Then if He says "no," I'm not disappointed.

Not Kleenex, Tissues

*"But avoid foolish and ignorant disputes, knowing
that they generate strife"*
(2 Timothy 2:23 NKJV).

While eating a meal at Kevin's house shortly before we married,
I discovered a quirk of his. When I asked, "Can you please
pass me the butter?" he corrected me, saying, "You mean the
margarine." I smiled, said "okay," and held out my hand for the
margarine.

A few hours later, I needed to blow my nose and asked where
he kept the Kleenex. "Oh, they're here in the linen closet. But
I don't call them Kleenex unless they are Kleenex brand. I call
them tissues." I forced my smile this time as I took the box of
tissues from his hand.

I wonder how many other things he's a stickler about, I
thought. *What if I refer to my tennis shoes and he says, "You*

really shouldn't call them tennis shoes unless you wear them to play tennis"? Or what if I ask him what record is playing and he says, "This isn't a record; it's a cassette tape"? I'm not sure I can live with someone who's so precise about things. It may drive me insane, and that looks bad for a preacher's wife.

Thankfully, these two items proved the only issues with Kev. Well, that was a lie. A few others have popped up, but he's repented of them since I've teased him so much. Wish I could've done that with some of our hair-splitting sheep.

At one of our first churches, Mrs. Keane fulfilled the role of rock in our shoe and thorn in our side all at once. She was not happy unless she was mad at someone. I once overheard her telling a Sunday school helper that she didn't know "what we're going to do with that young preacher if he doesn't shape up." Weak morals? Faulty doctrine? Lack of leadership skills? Nope. Mrs. Keane was beside herself over Kevin's lack of lawn-mowing skills. For shame.

Another time, she shook her boney finger in our faces because we were ill clad when we brought communion to her invalid son on a Sunday afternoon. It was July 4, 1976, our nation's bicentennial, and we'd decorated some matching T-shirts with iron-on transfers of Betsy Ross for the occasion. Mrs. Keane was incensed that we'd dressed inappropriately to serve the Lord's Supper. If Betsy herself had brought communion, I'm sure Mrs. Keane would've found her sleeves too poufy or her shoes too dusty.

One of our favorite legalists was a church musician, Sadie

Mill. I always felt Dill would have been a more appropriate name for this sour character, at least on Sunday mornings. No matter what songs we chose, Sadie refused to play anything faster than a funeral dirge. But when she sat down on that piano stool on Sunday nights, she became Sadie Sweet, relishing every arpeggio and grace note she could squeeze in. She rocked the stained glass right out of the windows with her snappy playing.

Nitpickers and gnat-strainers will drive us batty. They may even threaten the life of a congregation. If we let them. The best way to keep our sanity in the midst of these modern-day Pharisees is to follow Jesus' example: focus on the eternal. Keep preaching the kingdom and love of God. Keep following the Lord's leading, in spite of concern over lawn length, communion serving attire, or the speed of the music. And most of all, learn to laugh.

I sometimes laugh so hard, I need to wipe away my tears with a Kleenex—oops, I mean a tissue.

Two Scoops & a Sprinkle

❖ Although I emphasize laughter therapy to deal with legalists, there may be times when we need sterner measures. Loving, scriptural confrontation is never comfortable, but it may help free someone caught in the snare of legalism.

❖ On rare occasions, I've asked the Lord to remove a non-repentant troublemaker from a congregation. We still love and pray for them, but it seems unfair to sacrifice the life of the whole flock for one obstinate sheep.

❖ I must guard against legalism in my own life, lest I find myself with an eyeful of logs. Do I cling too much to my opinions? Am I unwilling to set minor issues aside for the sake of godly harmony? What areas in my heart do I need cleansed of Phariseeism?

What, No Worm?
(Candy's Apples)

"The Lord will guide you always; he will satisfy your needs in a sun-scorched land and will strengthen your frame. You will be like a well-watered garden, like a spring whose waters never fail"
(Isaiah 58:11 NIV).

My cousin Candy could hear two-year-old Nicky crying from across the huge lawn. Plopped under the apple tree, he clutched an apple in each dimpled fist while other preschoolers in her daycare munched contentedly.

"What's wrong with Nicky?" Candy asked her helper, Erin. "He sounds inconsolable."

"He's disappointed because all the other kids got worms in their apples and his are only fruit."

Laughter bubbled from Candy's lips. "I bet Dad never dreamed worm-free apples would bring such grief when he planted this tree!"

When Candy told me that story, I thought of my Heavenly Father. How many times have I wanted "worms" when He's given me sweet, nourishing fruit? Over my lifetime, I have cried to Him, gotten mad at Him, and even questioned His wisdom when He's said no to a direction I wanted to go. Later, I found He was protecting me from the "worms" of anguish or destructive consequences. He offered His love, joy, peace, patience, goodness, kindness, gentleness, faithfulness, and self-control: everything I would ever need to give me the life I wanted. Yet I have sat under the apple tree and bawled like a toddler because all I got was fruit.

Perhaps my Good Shepherd asked me to give up a habit I was comfortable with, one I saw no need to set aside. Did I insist on keeping my wormy apple because everyone else had one, and I didn't want to be different?

The apostle Paul was inspired to write, "For now we are looking in a mirror that gives only a dim (blurred) reflection" (I Corinthians 13:12a *Amplified Bible*). We may think someone's job, checkbook, or marriage is better than ours. We may fall into envy. Sometimes, God gives us insight into the true nature of a situation, revealing a worm or two we hadn't noticed. Other times, He expects us to trust His love for us. We must be content to know that if He refuses a request or asks us to give up a habit or relationship, it will ultimately make us happier and freer than if we'd kept it.

The more I read and meditate on God's Word, the more I'm convinced of the Father's love for me *personally*. Not only a blanket of love for mankind as a whole, but a custom-made love for me as a unique individual. His plan is for each of His children to hold a bright and happy future. If that means giving up a worm or two along the way, then I am going to be mature enough to say, "Okay, Papa, I know you love me and I trust you. What would you have me do?"

That kind of trust produces a sweeter, more fruitful life.

Two Scoops & a Sprinkle

❖ Most times, we know a besetting sin is keeping us from unbroken fellowship with God. But like Nicky, we're reluctant to let it go. The momentary fun it affords seems to fill a soulish need. But when trouble or sorrow comes because of sin, we realize that only God can fully satisfy our deepest longings.

❖ It's okay to say, "Lord, I know I'm hurting You and myself with this attitude (or behavior), but I can't stop on my own. Please intervene in my life so I can break free. I can't do this without You." This is called humility, and the Lord loves it. Now, prepare yourself for a miracle of grace.

❖ We can be tempted to think a brother or sister's faults are worse than ours. This gives us an open door to excuse our sinful habits. Don't fall prey to that deception. We need to pray for others to overcome their weaknesses, but be man or woman enough to own up to ours.

The Unrepentant Kitten

"The Lord is not slow in keeping his promise, as some
understand slowness. He is patient with you, not wanting
anyone to perish, but everyone to come to repentance"
(2 Peter 3:9 NIV).

Tigger loved the two and a half acres surrounding the church we pastored in central California. A little too much, if you want my opinion.

In the city we'd moved from, Tigger had spent the eight months of her life dodging cars, breathing smog, and cowering at the sound of sirens. Our new setting offered trees to climb, grass to run through, and a 4-H project heifer just over the neighbor's fence. A kitten's paradise. Especially a hunting kitten like Tigger.

When I left the parsonage for work each morning, I often discovered a lizard deposited on the front porch. I should say *lizard parts.* Tigger had thoughtfully removed the best portion for me, in case I wanted to take a snack to work but didn't have time to prepare it. We called them "front porch tails." I tried not to think about what she'd done with the other parts. Hunting reptiles was not the only item in her repertoire, however.

Tigger worked diligently to achieve the rank of #1 Rodent Exterminator for Santa Barbara County. Every mouse, gopher, and mole family in our area must've attended seventeen funerals in the two years we lived there. But I wondered why she felt compelled to add delivery service to her list of duties. If I was home alone and heard her scuffling on the porch, I made sure the door remained closed. I had discovered the hard way that "Catch the Cat with a Mouthful of Mouse" was not a fun inside game. Neither was her "Potluck Birdie Surprise."

An abundance of trees provided Tigger with her own feathery smorgasbord. This did not present a problem until one Saturday evening when the seniors held their monthly carry-in supper. Since it was a balmy night, they had propped open the fellowship hall door leading outside. Instead of a cool wind, Tigger breezed in, bringing her contribution to the potluck: a plump sparrow. She deposited it under a table, sunk her claws in without even a breath of thanks, and began her meal. The ladies setting tables were not amused.

"Oh, my heavens," shouted Mrs. Fry, "your cat just brought a bird in here. She's under that chair—quick, fetch me a broom, someone!"

With a bit of patience and finesse, I could have coaxed

Tigger out from under the table and escorted her outside. But Mrs. Fry was too squeamish to allow me the luxury of sweet talk and gentle nudges. After a loud "Shoo!" and a thump from the broom that allowed the bird to escape, Tigger exited the potluck in disgrace.

At home in our kitchen, I tried to sooth her ruffled fur with a spoonful of tuna and kitty-baby talk. "I'm sorry that mean lady hit you with her broom, honey," I cooed as I petted her. "Humans don't feel the same way cats do about birds—especially dead ones. I know all the trees are like a personal birdie smorgasbord," I said, "but you'll have to keep your dinners private from now on. Okay, Tiggie Wiggie?" She gave me a superior stare, put her nose in the air, and pranced away.

By the next morning, I'd forgiven and forgotten her offense of the previous night and let her out when I left for church. She didn't follow me, but climbed a tree to trick me into thinking she had plans to spend the morning bird watching. I should have guessed otherwise.

During the invitation hymn, Tigger snuck in through the open back door of the church. Before I could grab her, she zoomed up the center aisle, bounded across the stage, and dove into the baptistery behind the pulpit. I sighed in relief when I remembered we didn't keep it filled due to a plumbing leak.

Not one to let an opportunity pass, Kevin remarked, "Our cat may jump into the baptistery, but she refuses to repent. Unlike her, you have the opportunity to turn from sin and ask the Lord's forgiveness. Coming to Jesus is more than jumping into a baptistery. It involves a lifestyle of following after the Savior and allowing Him to be Lord of every area of your life."

Although I admired him for using this teachable moment, I couldn't stay to listen. I scurried behind the baptistery curtain, scooped up my unrepentant feline, and toted her home. Until her next misadventure. . . .

Two Scoops & a Sprinkle

❖ Pets can teach us much about our relationship with the Lord. A dog who eagerly obeys its master sets a sterling example of devotion and love. A cat like Tigger who attracts trouble reminds us of the Lord's unconditional grace.

❖ Tigger's jump into the baptistery formed a dramatic backdrop for Kevin's salvation appeal. Subtler teachable moments surround us every day, if we stay sensitive to them. Let's ask God to put words in our mouths to say the right things when opportunities arise.

❖ As a child, I thought repentance meant feeling sorry for your sin. I later discovered that Biblical repentance involves a change of heart and mind that leads to surrendering my will to God's.

I Don't Mind

"Cast all your anxiety on Him because he cares for you"
(1 Peter 5:7 NIV).

Ron discovered the phrase "I don't mind" when he was three. He used it often, at the most convenient times.

"Mommy, can I play in the sandbox?"

"No, Son, it's been raining all morning."

"I don't mind."

"It's time to take a bath, Ron. You'll be so dirty in a day or two that carrots will start sprouting out your ears."

"I don't mind."

"Just one more cookie, Dad?"

"No, Son, too many sweets can give you cavities."

"I don't mind."

There are days I would love to own that "I don't mind" spirit. When the church offerings are down, the parsonage carpet needs replacing, and Mrs. Persnickety is complaining for the ninety-ninth time about the newfangled praise music, I'd love to be able to dance through the frustration and sing, "I don't mind." Or when I'm concerned about my widowed mother two thousand miles from me, my car is making funny noises, or an odd-shaped bump shows up on my cat's neck, I'd enjoy adopting that "I don't mind" attitude.

I wish I could enroll in an eight-week course entitled "Care Casting," where a serene instructor with no worry lines between her brows would teach me how to stop fussing forever. At the end of the course, I'd take a three-question test on which I'd score 100 percent and receive my "Care Free" certificate. From that point forward, whenever Satan tempted me to fret, I'd point to the mahogany-framed document hanging on the wall and say, *"I don't mind. It's in God's hands. Now get out of here, you old liar."*

But sometimes I forget what I've learned.

I stumble, skinning my heart or breaking it into twenty-nine jagged pieces. Jesus never stomps over to where I've fallen, glares down, and says, "What is wrong with you? I've told you a thousand times that I will take care of you. Yet you insist on trying to fix situations your own way, ending up in trouble. Why won't you listen?"

Instead, He kneels down in the grime beside me and wipes the tears from my sodden cheeks with His heavenly handkerchief, woven of the softest angel hair. He hugs me tightly to His chest, where I can hear His heart drumming a love song with my name in the chorus. He lets me blub and blab as long as

I need, nodding in all the right places, never interrupting, just understanding.

When I'm through lamenting, Jesus lifts me to my feet and bandages my heart, beginning the process of putting it back together. Sometimes it takes a while. It always takes longer than I like.

He uses various kinds of glue: words from a song, a compliment from a dear friend, a Bible passage, a prayer spoken over me by my husband, a hilarious movie. He never rushes me to "get over it." He cares more about how the job is done than how long it takes. He uses all the resources I allow Him, to strengthen me for the next test, and the next.

Because, as you too have discovered, we never finish taking those pesky "Care Casting" classes. New tests pop up when we feel least equipped to take them. Our instructors are often people we'd rather not listen to. And there are no summer breaks.

These thoughts needn't worry us, though. As long as Jesus sits beside us—and He does—His love-inspired tutoring will see us through every test. Because we are always on His mind, we can say with Ron, "I don't mind."

Two Scoops & a Sprinkle

❖ Because God already knows our hearts, He does not need to test us. He will sometimes allow testing, however, so we can see areas we need to surrender to Him.

❖ The enemy keeps a profile on each of us, and knows our weakest spots. He loves to sneak in a horrible trial when we least expect it. The best way to be prepared for His nasty pop-quizzes is to keep studying the Text Book, so the answers will come quickly to mind.

❖ Jesus said, "Do not let your heart be troubled." We can speak to our hearts, telling them to trust in the Lord and not worry.

Secret Offerings

" 'But when you give to the needy, do not let your left hand
know what your right hand is doing, so that your giving may be
in secret. Then your Father, who sees what
is done in secret, will reward you' "
(Matthew 6:3-4 NIV).

Rats. I'd forgotten to bring my offering. As the communion
music ended, I opened my purse to find only a wheat back
penny. I'd saved wheat backs for years, hoping to cash them in
someday. I figured by the time I was eighty my collection would
be worth say, fifty cents or a dollar. My investment savoir faire
amazed me.

It's not that I begrudge you this wheat back, Lord, I thought.
But, what about the deacon who sees me put it in the plate? I'd
hate him to think I'm cheap. Since I'm the preacher's wife, I
should maintain a little dignity here, don't you think? Lord?

No answer.

Several months earlier, God had nudged me to bring an offering whenever I attended church. He didn't require an amount. He only asked that I bring something in addition to my tithe, *every time.*

I thought He was trying to teach me to show my appreciation for Him in a tangible way. But no. He had bigger plans.

The first few weeks, I obeyed with ease. I usually had an extra dollar or two in my wallet. If not, I could rummage around the house before church and find a bill or coin to bring.

My obedience soon grew horns of smugness. I hadn't told anyone except Kevin about my secret offerings. Not only was I giving extra each week, I was giving in secret. Wow. I impressed myself with my devotion to the Lord. Until the Sunday of the wheat back.

Lord, I'm the minister's wife. Won't my putting a penny in the plate set a poor example?

Still no answer. I sensed my Father was more interested in my obedience than in what Deacon Brown thought of me. So I slipped the penny onto the crimson felt and bowed my head, pretending to pray.

I'd love to tell you that since that day, one stranger after another has flagged me down to put hundred dollar bills into my hand. And that someone built us a new home on seven acres of wooded property within one hour's driving distance of our grandkids. But those would be lies.

Instead, I received a greater blessing. A corner of my heart was set free.

I've always longed to obey the Lord. Do whatever He told me, without argument, regardless of how I felt. I'd prayed many times, "Lord, give me an obedient heart. Help me follow You. Teach me Your ways." But I had a chain around my soul. I worried what people thought of me. Especially people in our church. Because we're called to lead them, I secretly believed that what they thought of me was important.

I cared too much for their respect. And not enough for God's applause. Now He was asking me to toss down my pride by giving him a penny. One cent. It was worth, at most, five cents to a coin dealer. Much more to Him who saw my secret motives.

At last, I relented. I let go of the wheat back, and my worry. As the penny landed on the pile of bills, my fear landed at Jesus' feet, replaced with surrender. A new joy burst into my heart: the joy of obedience.

If I ever become wealthy and the Lord asks me to give it all away, I trust I will obey without a blink. It's only money, after all. Not worth a cent compared to the offering of an obedient heart.

Two Scoops & a Sprinkle

❖ Although I've not grown rich from giving that one coin to the Lord, I've since found umpteen wheat back pennies. God isn't paying me back. He's saying, "Atta girl. I'm proud of you for obeying me."

❖ Jesus preached more about money than any other topic. Our attitude toward it mirrors the condition of our heart.

❖ Pride is not only self-centeredness. It can also take the form of fear. If I worry what others will think of me and say about me, I'm operating from pride. If I seek to please my Father, I'll hear, "Well done, good and faithful servant. Enter into the joy of your Lord." Obedience yields the richest joys.

Help Me!

"Yet the Lord longs to be gracious to you; he rises to show you
compassion. For the Lord is a God of justice.
Blessed are all who wait for him!"
(Isaiah 30:18 NIV).

On a Sunday afternoon when Esther was three, our little family
strolled down the mall. Estie held Daddy's hand on one side and
a bag of jellybeans in the other. When some candies tumbled
onto the brick walkway, Kev bent to pick them up. Estie rushed
ahead, adamantly saying, "NO. I can do it myself."

Kevin shrugged in my direction. "Oh, well. I tried."

"Kind of like how we treat God sometimes, isn't it?" I said.

Although I've grown up a thimbleful or so since then—at
least in years—I still try to clean up my own messes. I attempt
to solve problems in my own strength when God can solve them
much better. After several failed attempts, a cartoon light bulb
blinks on above my head and I realize, *Maybe I should have*

asked God to help me in the first place, instead of trying to achieve this all by myself. He DOES know more than I do, and He's been around a lot longer.

When I was very young, before I could read for myself, my daddy told me that his favorite Bible verse was "God helps those who help themselves." Then I grew up and discovered that verse was missing from the Bible. People who feel uncomfortable asking God for help manufactured Daddy's favorite verse, to affirm their self-reliance. In God's Word, self-reliance equals pride.

The most profound, inspired prayer anyone can pray is *"Help me, God."* That is in the Bible—all throughout it, in fact. You'll find it on the lips of heroes like Moses, Samson, David, Deborah, and Jesus. I decided I'd be wise to imitate them.

- When I can tell the conversation is turning into an argument, *Help me be kind.*
- When my hair wants to style itself and I am running late, *Help me get this messy mop to go in the right direction, please.*
- When I am stressing over a challenge at work or a personal problem baffles me, *Help me understand this, Lord.*
- When a friend is in trouble, *Help me say the right thing to comfort her.*
- When I don't know what direction to take in life, *Help me hear your voice, Lord.*

- When I'm on the phone with one of my kids who is 550 miles away and needs some heavy-duty advice, *Help me give them your divine wisdom, please.*

I ask God to help me cook, drive safely, listen attentively, do my job well, find items while shopping, keep a balanced perspective, choose what clothes to wear, have wisdom for my future, write encouragingly, sing well, understand people who don't think like I do, and everything in between. There is nothing too big and nothing too small to ask God. That's why He's in charge.

He longs to help us. He yearns to have pity on us, and He hears when we call to Him.

If we insist on picking up our own spilled candies, He will let us. He is a gentleman. However, it's much more fun to see how He invents ways to untie the tightest knots and un-pickle the stupidest situations we manage to get into!

Let's not be like a stubborn three-year-old now that we know the truth: God does not help those who help themselves. He helps those who ask for it.

Two Scoops & a Sprinkle
- ❖ If we refuse to go to God for help, does this mean we think we can manage better without Him?
- ❖ God doesn't usually give us help in the ways we expect. He has a billion ideas up His sleeves that we've never considered. Let Him decide how to give us a hand. Our job is to ask.
- ❖ Occasionally, God will send the help we need in the form of a person we dislike. Can we receive the present with grace, even if its package isn't fun?

The Brouhaha Twins

"Put on the full armor of God so that you can take your stand against the devil's schemes. For our struggle is not against flesh and blood, but against the rulers, against the authorities, against the powers of this dark world and against the spiritual forces of evil in the heavenly realms"
(Ephesians 6:11-12 NIV).

When we exchanged wedding rings thirty-something years ago, we were stupid. We both thought the other was the best invention since programmable coffee makers. Then we went on our honeymoon and got in our first big fight. Seems we had differing opinions on how to sing a song we were rehearsing for the following Sunday (can you believe we practiced singing on our honeymoon? I told you we were stupid). Since then we've had one brouhaha after another.

Lately, *brouhaha* has made it to the #3 spot on the list of most-used words in our household. According to some overweight book we own, it means "to dramatize; to overreact; to throw a conniption fit over things inconsequential," or something like that. If I could find the book, I'd quote it verbatim, but I'll save the topic of clutter for another time.

We do not plan our brouhahas. They sneak up on us suddenly, like a taxes-due reminder. We've gotten upset over the consistency of spaghetti sauce, how close to have the oven rack while broiling chicken, the most efficient leaf-raking technique, and my personal favorite: "Why are you just staring at your wife who is struggling with a difficult task when you could be pitching in and helping her?"

We don't throw fits over trifles. Oh, no. Our arguments are wisely spent. Politics, spiritual matters, and the economy rarely merit an argument. But, spaghetti sauce and chicken chests . . .

It only took me six weeks to figure out why this is happening now: we are studying *Conflict-Free Living* in our ladies' Sunday school class. It's a marvelous, inspiring book about living in peace with everyone from spouse to boss. Of course, we get to test it out every Monday, Tuesday, Wednesday, etc. I have a feeling I'm not getting the highest grade in the class. And I'm the teacher.

Unless you live in a cave, you've noticed that whatever area of spiritual growth you're focusing on gets tested. I don't believe God does the testing (see James 1:13). God already knows what's in our heart. It's that pesky devil, the enemy of our souls, who wants to ruin our lives. He hates it when we study God's Word and seek to grow, so he tempts us in the areas we're currently working on.

This turns to our benefit, because we see that filthy pride we thought we'd repented of on the honeymoon. How terribly painful to realize it's still there, oozing out our hearts and eventually our mouths.

But if we don't see it, we'll never understand what's holding us back from the intimacy with God we long for. It takes the searchlight of God's Word to expose sin. Until then, we can keep it hidden, calling it an "inherited trait," or blaming someone else for it.

When we mature enough to admit we are wrong, we're set free to turn to the only One who can help us out of our mess—our loving Father. How elated He is when we humble ourselves and admit we need Him to fix us. Now He can gently, mercifully change us from selfish little brouhaha brats to stable Christians.

Say, would you like to come over for some spaghetti this weekend? We will be making two kinds of sauce. . . .

Two Scoops & a Sprinkle

❖ We build a marriage as a contractor builds a home: one brick and board at a time. When we expect instant success to overcome differences, we set ourselves up for disappointment.

❖ Learning to resolve areas of disagreement can be painful. No one enjoys saying, "I messed up. Please forgive me. Let's find a way to make this work." But it beats staying in our messes.

❖ Every marriage experiences conflict. The enemy targets pastors and their spouses more than lay people because we are influencers. When we keep the armor of God in place, we keep the devil under our feet.

Jumping Bales with Jesus

"'When he has brought out all his own, he goes on ahead of them, and his sheep follow him because they know his voice'"
(John 10:4 NIV).

A pastor can learn a lot by listening. Kevin is one of the rare preachers who still calls on people in their homes. Some feel it an intrusion of their privacy or their favorite TV show, and don't invite him in. Others welcome a visit from the pastor and a chance to share their lives. Andy was one of the welcomers.

As a young man, Andy had worked with sheep. He and the other ranch hands had made a fun discovery, which he related to Kevin. "If one sheep is first to do something, the others will follow it in minute detail, no matter how idiotic or dangerous it is.

"A sheep can jump three feet in the air to sail over a bale of hay" he continued, "and every sheep to follow him will jump exactly three feet when approaching the same bale. If you put a second bale on top of the first one, all the sheep will jump only three feet up, plowing into the second bale."

When Kevin told me Andy's story, we laughed at the sheep's stupidity. Until I realized how often I behave like them. For instance . . .

Mrs. Bible Study Expert says if I want to be Mrs. Exemplary Christian, I must read the Bible through every year with her plan. I dive in with intensity, only to crash in disappointment when I fail to keep up.

Ms. House Cleaning Expert says if I buy her magic sink-cleaning cloths, I will be motivated to keep my house pristine. I sign up for her daily e-mails and purchase my dirt-busting cloths. When my inbox overflows and I yell at my husband for leaving dishes in my shiny sink, I weep in frustration at my backward priorities.

Mr. Ministry Expert tells me I need to mentor a group of five to seven people for a period of one year, teaching them all I've learned of Jesus, and then send them out to mentor others. It takes me six months to find five people willing to sit and listen to me blather about my life once each week, but I manage it. When I'm sick to my stomach from hearing myself talk about myself, I realize I'm the one needing the mentoring.

All these experts—these lead sheep—flew over that bale. Why didn't it work when I copied them? Because I wasn't designed to follow other sheep.

My bale may be taller or my hooves smaller than the lead sheep. The Shepherd could be calling me to jump a different way. But I see how simple that lead sheep makes it look. And I've read her newest book, *Bale Jumping Fast and Easy*. So here I jump, a carbon copy of her.

If I crash and break a nose or an ego, I can't blame my Shepherd. He tried to direct me, guiding my steps with His tender words, but I ignored Him. I was intent on following that lead sheep.

Dear friends, each lamb's path is unique. If we try to follow another sheep, we will not fulfill the Good Shepherd's plan for our own lives. He knows best what the custom-made design is for each of his beloved lambs. Only as we get alone with Him, asking for His divine wisdom and seeking His special purpose for us, will we sail over those bales of discouragement, fear, and closed doors.

I know what your answer will be. Still, I must ask: *Will you follow the lead sheep, or chase after the Shepherd?*

Two Scoops & a Sprinkle

❖ Jesus knew how tempted we'd be to follow other sheep instead of Him. So He gave us the Holy Spirit. One of the Spirit's jobs is to guide us into God's perfect plan for our individual lives. The more we ask, "What would you have me do, Lord?" the more victories we'll experience.

❖ It's okay to listen to others' counsel and success stories. They can help us avoid defeat, and aid us in spiritual growth. It's not okay to follow their methods in detail without asking God for His input.

❖ We need to exercise caution when advising others regarding a non-Scriptural matter. It's best to say, "This method worked for me, but you need to seek direction from the Word and the Lord before trying it."

A Radical Secret for Forgiving Sister Sourpuss and Brother Barracuda

"'But I say to you who hear: Love your enemies, do good to those who hate you, bless those who curse you, and pray for those who spitefully use you'"
(Luke 6:27-28 NKJV).

Many years ago, I learned a secret that's enabled me to forgive even the most hateful people.

Lynette, a speaker at a ladies' meeting, shared the story of her drug-addict son-in-law. She'd grown into a bundle of rage over the suffering he'd inflicted on their family. She wanted to forgive, but was imprisoned by her hatred. Then God taught her a ridiculous method for setting her heart free of bitterness. Her secret? "Bless them."

When I heard this, I inwardly sniffed in contempt. *That's nothing new*, I thought.

As if Lynette had read my thoughts, she said, "When Jesus told us to bless those who persecute us, He wasn't telling us to say a few wimpy 'God bless thems.' The word *bless* means 'to speak highly of, to commend, to give credit to.' When we bless someone, we are wishing them well." But she didn't stop there.

"Bless everything you can imagine about the person who wronged you. Bless their hair, so it won't fall out. Bless their driveway, that it won't have cracks. Bless their lawn, that it won't turn brown. Get radical. The blessing will soon flush the hate from your heart, and you'll find forgiveness in its place."

The following week, I found an opportunity to practice Lynette's method.

I needed to say no to Agnes, a lady who wanted a favor. I tried to explain in a loving way why I must let her down, but she refused to understand, spewing harsh words at me. As my heart lay bloodied and bruised, Lynette's words about blessing came to mind.

I blessed Agnes for a while before going to a baby shower that evening. "Lord, I bless Agnes's toenails, that they never become ingrown. I bless her kids, that they never sass her. I bless her roof, that no shingles fall off." I laughed at these silly ideas, but my heart still felt like a stone in my chest.

While at the shower, I became distracted with having fun. But the minute I reached my car, memories of Agnes's harsh words bombarded my mind. So I blessed her some more on the drive home. "God, I bless Agnes's knees, that they never get warts. I bless her husband's job, that he gets regular raises. I bless her cooking, that it never makes anyone sick." Still, when I went to bed that night, the pain was ready to explode in my stomach.

I grumbled to the Lord, "This blessing business doesn't seem to be working." But I kept at it, stretching my brain to come up with clever ways to bless Agnes.

"Jesus, I bless Agnes's washer, so it'll never leak. I bless her roses, that they'll never have aphids. I bless her scalp, to be free of dandruff." This was starting to get ridiculous.

When I woke the next morning, the first thing to tsunami into my mind was the memory of Agnes's abuse. But instead of the heavy ache filling my heart, it was flooded with a calm, divine peace. I could think of what Agnes said with no pain or anger—I was free!

I realized then that this was not Lynnette's method. It was Jesus'. He told us to bless our enemies not for their benefit alone, but also for ours. Something miraculous takes place in our hearts when we extend grace to one who has wounded us. We not only become a catalyst for their healing, but our own souls are restored in the process.

I've used this radical secret to forgiveness repeatedly, with phenomenal results. No matter how silly I may feel as I bless Sister Sourpuss's toenails or Brother Barracudas' toast, I'm sticking with something that works every time. I may be ditzy, but I'm not stupid.

Two Scoops & a Sprinkle

❖ Although blessing someone who mistreated us is one of the hardest things we may ever do, it is easier than being captive to bitterness and misery.

❖ Don't feel like it? Ignore your feelings, which aren't a reliable source of God's leading, and do it anyway.

❖ When we choose to bless rather than curse hateful people, we are stepping up to Jesus' level of love. He laid down His life for His enemies, many of whom later became His followers.

The Grave of the Unknown Cat

"I cry aloud to the Lord; I lift up my voice to the Lord for mercy. I pour out my complaint before him; before him I tell my trouble"
(Psalm 142:1-2 NIV).

Grief twisting his face, Kevin slumped in the doorway of the church basement, where I'd retreated to pray. His sigh filled the room.

"What happened, honey? You look like you lost your best friend."

He winced. "No . . . but you . . . Oh, Jeanette, I'm so sorry."

"What? Who?"

"Diana found your kitten in the road, apparently hit by a car. I didn't think you'd want to identify the body. I just finished burying her."

Wilting into his arms, I sobbed, "Oh, no, not Judy!"

Our neighbor Diana had bestowed Judy on us when we moved from L.A. to Illinois a few months earlier to pastor a rural church. Hearing how I'd carted our other two felines in under-the-seat carriers on the plane trip here, Diana jumped to the crazy conclusion I liked cats. After we'd settled in, she offered me the pick of her litter.

Judy, a luxuriant ball of gleaming white/gray fur, had held her dainty pink nose and bushy tail aloft. She paraded around Diana's living room with the air of a princess in training. We bonded on the spot.

Although my older cats snubbed the newcomer, Judy's spunk helped cure my homesickness for friends left behind. We played and cuddled through gray autumn days. I spoke to her in my silly, high-pitched "kitty-witty" voice reserved only for special fur babies. I even purchased a brush to groom her glossy tresses, something I'd never indulged in before.

Now she was gone.

After Kevin left, I paced and wept, anguish clawing at my gut. "I don't understand, Lord. We came two thousand miles to pastor Your people. We took huge pay cuts to move here. I would think You'd want to reward us. Now my baby is dead. Why me? Why this? Help me understand."

It took a full twenty minutes to blubber my complaints. Finally, I told the Lord, "Okay. I don't serve You because You make my life perfect and fulfill my every wish. I serve You because You are God. I don't understand why Judy was killed today, but I will love You no matter what. I'm still upset, but someday I'll smile again." Taking a deep, jagged breath, I started home.

I took my time crossing the parking lot from the church to the parsonage, my eyes on the gravel. But as I neared our driveway, I spied a flash of gray and white fur streaking across the lawn, bounding toward me. "Judy," I cried, scooping her into my arms, "it wasn't you after all!" Feeling like I'd received my child back from the dead, I purred my thanks to God as I ran inside to find Kevin.

"Honey, look who's here—a feline version of Lazarus!"

Kev did not share my excitement. "Then who's the kitten I buried in the backyard twenty minutes ago? It took me forever to dig that hole. Since we don't have a shovel, I had to use the garden spade."

Although I empathized with his calloused hands and sore shoulders, I couldn't help grinning as I nuzzled Judy's cheek. "I don't know, Kev. It must've been a stray resembling Judy. At least it received a proper burial. Shall we plant some flowers in honor of The Unknown Cat?"

He grunted. "Only if you dig the holes!"

Two Scoops & a Sprinkle

❖ Sometimes we take on the notion that God owes us for whatever we've given up to follow Him. The truth is, if not for His sacrifice, we'd have no one to follow.

❖ When we have a complaint, God appreciates honesty. We can't receive help from Him if we refuse to admit that we're angry or disappointed. Once we uncork our grievance, He can go to work to help us fix it. Until then, we're left to wimpy human solutions.

❖ I believe God gave us pets to fill a valid need for companionship and nurturing. People who own pets live longer, experience less stress, and enjoy life more.

Take a Closer Look

*"And he is the head of the body, the church; he is the beginning
and the firstborn from among the dead, so that in everything he
might have the supremacy. For God was pleased
to have all his fullness dwell in him"*
(Colossians 1:18-19 NIV).

Our stomachs competed with each other for the loudest grumble
in Indianapolis. I scanned the sign at the mall entrance for a
likely restaurant.

"Peking Duck. That sounds good, but kind of expensive. Do
you feel like Chinese, Kev?"

"That'd be fine, but the sign actually says *Parking Deck*,
Jeanette. I don't think we'd find much to eat there!"

I simply hadn't looked close enough at the sign.

Some people think they know what the Bible and Christianity
are all about because they have a friend or two who are Christians
or they've been to church a few times. Perhaps they grew up

in church, but never progressed in their relationship with God. I had been one of these "glancers at God," even though I had become a Christian at age eight.

From the time I was ten days old, my parents brought me to church. At age seven, I listened as my Sunday school teacher related Jesus' miracles to us. I fell in love with this God-man who could walk on water, heal lepers, and raise the dead.

After I was baptized on Mother's Day, 1964, a hunger to read the Bible overtook me. I wanted to tell all my friends about Jesus, and my newfound faith. However, I still didn't really know Him, as you know a friend or a family member. Until I took a closer look.

Like many adolescents, my teen years were fraught with insecurities. The fact that I grew up in an alcoholic home and my daddy had died when I was ten didn't help. But one summer I met a man, the friend of a friend, who saw my blatant need for a deeper relationship with God. He challenged me to read Psalm 139 until I knew in my heart—not just my head—that God loved me unconditionally, and was personally interested in me and everything about me.

I took that gentleman's challenge, and from that time forward, gradually and steadily, my life has turned around. I went from Psalm 139 to other places like Romans 8, John 15, and the entire book of Colossians. I took a closer look at this Jesus I had given my life to, and found out that He was more than simply a man who did miracles. He was everything I had ever needed and longed for. He not only filled the universe with His glory, He filled my sagging soul with His kindness and patience. And a genuine love that would not abandon me.

The more I looked closely at Him in His Word, the more real He became to me. My healer when I'm sick. My deliverer when I'm beset with habits or sin. My shepherd when I don't know which way to turn. My joy when I am depressed. My strength when I can't go another step. My best friend when I feel too alone against the world and the devil. My grace and wisdom when I don't have the wits to solve a problem.

Looking back, I realize that had the final trumpet blown before the Psalm 139 challenge, I would have gone to heaven. However, the journey there wouldn't have been as enjoyable. My relationship with Jesus up to that time had been similar to being married to someone with whom you never eat a meal. Or perhaps like trying to eat a fancy Chinese meal at a parking lot. You can manage it, but it's not much fun.

Don't settle for anything less than the best meal you can get out of God. Take a closer look at Him today. Dig into His Word, fellowship with Him in prayer, and find a Jesus who is everything you will ever need.

Two Scoops & a Sprinkle

- ❖ We will never get to the place where we can say, "I know God fully."
- ❖ Don't be afraid to challenge someone to go deeper in their walk with the Lord. You'll be doing them an enormous favor.
- ❖ God wants us to know Him so we'll not only value His marvelous character, but also so that He can bless us with His continual presence in our lives.

A Hairy Deal

*"When Jesus heard what had happened, he withdrew by
boat privately to a solitary place. Hearing of this, the crowds
followed him on foot from the towns. When Jesus landed and
saw a large crowd, he had compassion on them
and healed their sick"*
(Matthew 14:13-14 NIV).

Tabitha had mastered the face-powdering method quite nicely
for a three-year-old. She'd ask the candidate to squat down, and
then she'd rub the powder sponge around the compact a time or
two, and gently pat the forehead, nose, cheeks, and chin. After
the church service one Sunday, she had done this with Aunt
Jackie's powder on several agreeable grown-ups. Everyone
found delight in her sweet little ritual. Until my husband became
her next client.

Tabbi naively asked him if he'd like his face powdered. He
chuckled as he bent down and closed his eyes. The child was

unprepared for what faced her, however. With sponge poised in her petite hand and question marks in her eyes, she looked up at me, shrugged and said, "Him have hair on him cheeks!"

Discovering that not all faces are created equal made Tabitha pause to rethink her procedure. It took just a few seconds for her to adjust her strategy, only powdering Kevin's nose and forehead, leaving out the hairy places. As she closed the compact, she smiled with satisfaction, unaware that she had practiced a very mature attitude: flexibility.

Wouldn't it be fun and relaxing to live like that?

I am famous for setting goals and making lists of things to accomplish. The challenge comes when God or someone else steps in with a "hairy" delay. I'm forced to trade in my plan and become flexible in less time than it takes to powder my face.

I plan to spend the evening writing or reading, and then my husband asks me to accompany him on a hospital visit. How do I respond?

Or I arrange a great dinner party with several friends, then burn the spaghetti and overcook the garlic bread. Can I devise a Plan B and still keep smiling?

And the real biggie of hairy delays: people who don't behave the way I want. I expect an individual to respond in a certain way, and they do just the opposite, ruining my idea or project. Does this cause me to melt down, or can I deal with it in a mature manner and stay happy?

I love the story of how Jesus turned an interrupted plan into a miracle. He and His friends had worked to the edge of exhaustion, and needed a vacation. He called them away from the throng to rest at a lakeside retreat. When the crowd saw where they were headed, they followed, bringing all their sick friends and relatives.

Did Jesus demand His right to some much-earned privacy and relaxation? No. He was "moved with compassion, and healed their sick."

Perhaps the enemy had planned this detour as a temptation for Jesus to lose His temper and ruin His shining example as God in the flesh. Perhaps it was simply a case of insensitivity on the crowd's part. After all, Jesus was a celebrity.

Whatever the cause of the distraction, Jesus followed His Father's plan, setting aside His own goals to help others. Because God says you reap whatever you sow (Galatians 6:7), I'm confident that He rewarded Jesus with a vacation. You can't do things God's way and lose.

I hope the next time I make a plan or set a goal and someone interrupts it, I'll have the maturity to be flexible and find an alternative arrangement. Tabbi and Jesus would.

Two Scoops & a Sprinkle

❖ Lowering our expectations of others is a great way to show flexibility, especially if we lean toward idealism.

❖ Because Jesus always listened for the Father's guidance, He was never caught off guard. This is how he avoided the devil's traps.

❖ Plans and goals are meant to be tools, not tyrants.

The Empty Box

"Through the Lord's mercies we are not consumed, because
His compassions fail not. They are new every morning;
great is Your faithfulness"
(Lamentations 3:22-23 NKJV).

When my husband carefully removed the tape from his second-to-last Christmas gift, mindful to save the shimmering red paper, I smiled in anticipation. He always asks for small items like CDs and DVDs, but I like to wrap them in large boxes. That way I can use more paper. Those big packages look so festive under the tree, mirroring the colored lights.

This box was one of the biggest.

"It feels kind of light," he said as he lifted the lid. He peered down at a single sheet of beige tissue paper, the kind they put in with shoes. "Oh," he said, his eyes questioning mine.

"What?" I hollered above Burl Ives' "Holly Jolly Christmas," and gazed into the empty box. "Umm…it's empty."

My mind spun. Could someone have broken into the house and stolen a gift from under the tree? Nah. Anyone who did that would take the entire box, not just remove the gift, and then re-wrap it to cover their crime. Besides, what kind of stupid criminal would only take one gift among dozens?

Then it must have been . . . Oh dear.

I giggled like a three-year-old caught sneaking candy from the stockings, and scratched my burning forehead. My whole face was burning. "I'm so sorry, honey. In my holiday frenzy, I must have wrapped an empty box, thinking I had put a gift in it."

I recalled the morning two weeks earlier when Kev was gone to Bible study. I had decided this was my best opportunity to wrap his presents. The eight-foot long kitchen counter was my workstation, drowning in gift bags, paper, boxes, tags, and ribbons. I must've got distracted by the phone ringing or a chocolate cupcake calling to me.

Kevin laughed as the limp sheet of tissue hung from his fingers. "It's okay, Jeanette. I have so many other nice gifts here. Don't worry about it."

But I was embarrassed. "I feel so awful—it wasn't a practical joke or anything. I just didn't know what I was doing."

He laughed again. His throaty chuckle was like a pat on the back, reassuring me that he knew it was just an oversight. He understands me.

I may disappoint him, hurt him, even anger him, but he keeps laughing at my ditzy doings, always returning to his deep well of unconditional love.

He reminds me of the Lord.

I used to wonder if God would tire of my shenanigans. I knew He offered fresh starts to His children, but I worried that I'd wear out His mercy.

I kept peering into the same empty boxes of stinky attitudes, willfulness, and impatience, saying, "Sorry, I just didn't know what I was doing." Surely, He'd get tired of hearing that excuse, and shut the book of *Graces for Goofballs* one last time, demanding that I grow up or He'd kick me out of His family.

Yet, He never has. For almost fifty years, He's been forgiving me, teaching me how to follow Him, and helping me forgive myself. He gives me a new empty box each morning, believing that I have what it takes to fill it with something worthwhile to give back to Him. It's His eternal belief in me that gives me hope for my tomorrows. He understands me. And He loves me in spite of it.

I have a feeling He understands you, too.

Two Scoops & a Sprinkle

❖ Knowing that Jesus believes in us more than we do in Him gives us courage to stay in the race despite our stumbles.

❖ Embarrassment can be useful, if it shows us where we need to change. Or, it can just make us feel silly. Either way, it helps to laugh at ourselves.

❖ The Lord always has more mercy than we have mistakes, since he cooks up a fresh batch every morning.

Baby Plans

"Every good gift and every perfect gift is from above, and comes down from the Father of lights, with whom there is no variation or shadow of turning"
(James 1:17 NKJV).

"I want another baby, Lance."

My boss's wife adored their tween-agers, Nancy and Paul, but longed for a wee one to nurture. For months, Lance had resisted her pleas. "Sonya, we have the perfect family: a boy and a girl. Let's be content with that. Besides, I'll be forty in a year. I don't want people thinking I'm my kid's grandfather at her high school graduation."

Sonya was undaunted. Bit by "the baby bug," she persisted in her heart's desire for one more child. And a recent miscarriage had made her more determined than ever to give Nancy and Paul a baby sister or brother.

Finally, Lance concocted a plan he was sure would discourage her. "All right, we can try one last time. But it must be a girl, she must be born before my fortieth birthday, and you need to have her on a Saturday, so I don't have to take off work to go to the hospital with you."

"Agreed," said Sonya, humming to herself as she thumbed through a Babies R Us catalog. Lance rolled his eyes as he left the room.

Nine months later, he was jolted awake when a finger gouged him in the rib. "Are you ready to go have this baby?" Sonya said. That afternoon, Tiffany June made her appearance. It was a Saturday, December 13, two days before Lance's fortieth birthday.

When Lance told me this story, I asked him if Sonya had prayed that he agree to another baby, or about the timing of Tiffany's birth. "Not that I know of," he said.

What? This really messes with my theology. I want people to have exactly what they want, when they want it, only if they have asked God for it. I certainly don't believe luck had anything to do with Tiffany's birth, so that leaves only one other answer: God did this as a favor to Lance and Sonya, simply because He loves them and wanted to bless them. Period.

Why does this bother me? Because I want my teeter-totter balanced. If I obey the Lord and honor Him with my life, I expect Him to answer outrageous prayers like a girl baby born on a certain day before her daddy's 40th birthday. But if a person who wants something a specific way gets it without even asking

God, what does that tell me?

Not what you might think. Not that it doesn't pay to serve God, or that we shouldn't pray for what we want and need, but simply this: God is God—He can do whatever He wants. And I believe it tickled Him to give Lance and Sonya exactly what they wanted, because He likes to make people happy. He is a good God who does favors for everyone, not only those who ask.

Here's a final thought. If God gave someone the desire of their heart when they didn't even ask Him, how much more would He give His own child who comes boldly to His throne and makes their requests known? Kinda makes you want to expect a lot more out of Him, doesn't it?

Two Scoops & a Sprinkle

❖ If someone told you that God would supply your basic needs but nothing more, they need to read Psalm 37:4 and Romans 8:32.

❖ It makes God happier to give us the good things we ask for than it makes us to receive them. Make God's day—ask Him for a favor. But don't stop there. Find out if He wants a favor from you, too. Then listen for His answer.

❖ When we ask God for the seemingly impossible, we aren't offending Him. But we might if we only ask Him for small things.

Beware of Moths and Sligs

"Words kill, words give life; they're either poison or fruit—you choose"
(Proverbs 18:21 The Message).

From the open kitchen window, I heard Esther and Ron playing in the sandbox on our patio. Ron was buzzing his Little People bus through the trails he'd made in the damp sand.

"Now, Ron," began five-year-old Esther, her tone full of caution, "if you ever go on a real bus, make sure you sit way in the back."

"Why?" asked Ron.

Estie's voice became dark with caution: "Because if a moth or a slig (her word for slug) comes in the front, you can run out the side door before it gets to you."

Ron stayed his usual calm self. "What will it do if it gets me?"

"Well, the moth will bite all your clothes off. I'm not sure what the slig will do, but you just better sit in the back like I said!"

Although Esther's motive was protecting her younger brother from harm, I wondered where she'd picked up the idea that moths would gobble your clothes down to the zippers.

Perhaps she'd overheard Kevin and me talk about putting moth cakes in her closet so her clothes wouldn't be ruined. *That's how rumors get started,* I chuckled to myself.

In thirty-plus years of ministry, we've had to dispel a few rumors of our own. Shortly after we were married, during our BC (Before Children) days, we moved from our first pastorate to a church several hours away. One day a package arrived from one of our former "sheep," an elderly lady we'd grown close to. When I opened it and saw the lovely pale green and yellow crocheting, I squealed with delight. "Oooh, a lap robe. How thoughtful of Rita. She must have known it was colder down here than in Fresno."

Then we saw them: silky pastel green and yellow ribbons on each corner of my new blanket. "Um, Jeanette, I don't think covering our laps was what Rita had in mind when she made that. I imagine it's meant to cover a baby."

"Oh dear," I moaned. "I wonder how she got the idea we were expecting?"

I sat down that moment and wrote her a sincere thank you note for all the work and love she'd put into our "lap robe," explaining that we weren't planning our family just yet, but when we did, she'd be one of the first to know.

Do you wonder how rumors get started? Are people bored and long to stir up some excitement, so they make up a shocking story? Do they see something that looks suspicious, and don't bother to ask the people involved what's really going on? Or, like Estie and Rita, do they misunderstand something they've heard?

Regardless of the reason for a rumor's beginning, we children of God must not be guilty of spreading questionable news about a person, group, or business. It's important that we go to the source of the rumor and find out the truth, so we can stop it if it's gossip.

We can ruin a person's reputation or cause a panic by negative, deadly words. Or, we can lift someone's broken spirit with positive, life-giving words. We're not bringing death or life to only those to whom we speak. Our words bring curses or blessings to our own hearts as well.

Next time you hear something that sounds a little juicy, let it stop with you. Those sligs and moths may be listening, and we wouldn't want them to get the wrong idea.

Two Scoops & a Sprinkle

❖ If it's none of my business, it qualifies as gossip.

❖ God created with words. Jesus healed, commanded nature, and raised the dead with words. Words are containers of power. Act like God; use your words for life and blessing.

❖ Some of the most nourishing words we can say: "Thanks," "Forgive me," and "I love you."

The Hormone Bomber

"Though the Lord is on high, he looks upon the lowly,
but the proud he knows from afar"
(Psalm 138:6 NIV).

I'm not the rebellious type. I went through that stage as a
teenager. It was as much—or more—of a nightmare for me as
it was for my parents. When I was seventeen, the Lord grabbed
my heart and tucked it into His. From then on, I realized that
pushing the limits, thinking I was above the rules, and making
others wait on me were nothing but pride. God hates pride. So,
most days I try to be humble. This way He doesn't have to come
looking for me.

However, I got myself into an interesting little mess recently
at the airport. Not on purpose. I just didn't realize how big of a
no-no I was committing.

"Will you step over here, please, ma'am?"

I looked up in shock. That solemn voice had risen above

the murmurs of dozens of travelers in the security station, and targeted me. Me? I glanced at the blue-clad security officer, raised my eyebrows, and met her cold gaze and definite nod. She motioned me inside the body scanner, which resembled a life-sized Barbie doll package. "Stand on the yellow footprints and lift your hands above your head, please. Now clasp them together and hold still." I was thankful I had decided to use twenty-four-hour deodorant.

What had aroused suspicions about me? I wondered. Surely not the three herbal hormone tablets in my pocket, half the size of a cell phone battery. I'd read the sign that said "PLEASE REMOVE ALL OBJECTS FROM YOUR POCKETS" when we entered the security checkpoint, but I figured this meant keys, pens, and pocketknives. My idea of ALL must be different from theirs.

"Do you have something in your right front pocket, ma'am?" Her voice was kind but firm. I didn't know whether to laugh in her face, look for the candid camera, or play the straight lady. I chose the latter.

"Yes, I have three hormone tablets."

She wasn't laughing, so I knew I'd made the right choice. "Please take them out and place them on your palm."

I gazed down at my dinky drugs as she inspected them, and allowed myself half a smile. "Do you consider these a threat?"

"The scanner can't tell what an image is—it only detects something in your pocket. Step over here, please." As she explained the pat-down process she was about to put me through,

I nodded. I knew she was only doing her job, a mostly unpleasant one. She didn't need my sarcasm and anger making it harder.

When she told me I was free to go and could board the plane, I sighed in relief. I would've hated to miss my brother's funeral in California because I broke a major law about not allowing hormones to board a plane.

But I still say the entire airline industry had better be happy I take those hormones, and thank the Lord I remembered to put the afternoon dosage in my pocket. The skies would not be very friendly if I had tucked those babies away in my suitcase.

And I don't think God was a bit ticked off with me for breaking the rules this one time. Even if the airlines haven't figured it out, He knows—we have yet to see the wrath of a bomber compared to the desperation of a woman without her hormones.

Two Scoops & a Sprinkle

❖ Although some of us never put our hands on our hips and shout, "NO!" we mask our rebellion in a thousand smaller ways.

❖ People in authority don't always like being there. We can make their jobs easier, and be a sweet witness for the Lord, by cooperating.

❖ Humility is walking in the truth. And the truth is, no one is more important than another is. If I think I'm above the rules, I'm acting in pride.

Buttons

"Do not be like the horse or the mule, which have no understanding but must be controlled by bit and bridle or they will not come to you"
(Psalm 32:9 NIV).

When I climbed into the saddle for the first time in more than forty years, I felt confident and secure. Until the blue-eyed, baby-face wrangler corrected me.

"Don't let Buttons eat. She's supposed to be working. If she tries that again, jerk her reins straight up, to make her uncomfortable." I failed to tell him it was too late—while he'd been saddling horses for the other fourteen riders, Buttons had stripped half the hillside of grass.

During the hour-long ride, another wrangler barely out of high school used me as an example of what not to do. "Buttons is thrashing her head around because she's agitated. You need to pull the reins back toward your belly, not straight up into the air."

I whined, "But the other boy—I mean man—told me to jerk it up, so she wouldn't keep eating!"

"Yes, she likes to eat. But you need to show her you're in charge, or she'll take advantage of you."

Now I was as confused as a pogo stick at a triathlon. Jerk the reins up to keep your horse from eating; jerk the reins back to keep your horse from getting agitated. I wanted to jerk the person who gave this ornery horse to wimpy me.

I never did excel at discipline. One day I let my kids eat Lucky Charms, skip their baths, and stay up till ten. The next day I yelled, "We eat too much junk around here; have this carrot stick and like it. Is that dirt I see behind your ears? Baths twice a day from now on. You have dark circles under your eyes; bedtime is now 7:00 p.m."

My Who's in Charge Meter kept changing its mind. I couldn't seem to strike a balance between allowing the kids to be kids and setting healthy boundaries. Riding Buttons was a thorny reminder of my inability to take charge without being a dictator.

Although the stinging sensation in my eyes threatened to turn to tears, I managed to swallow my embarrassment and pretend I was having fun. As I dismounted, I joked that riding Buttons was like trying to get a two-year old to cooperate. Everyone laughed, and I snuffled the tears away.

But later that evening on my way back to the cabin, the Lord surprised me with a prickly thought. "You think Buttons was hard to manage today, Jeanette? She reminds me of you. Always champing at the bit to eat when I need you to work, trying to lead me rather than following. Yet I continue to be patient with you, gently guiding you with my spirit. I will never give up on you, My child."

Wow. No wonder He's God and I'm not. While I'm ready to pitch a plan, a project, or even a person because I'm impatient with things not going the right way—which usually means MY way—the Lord is barely tapping into His storehouse of longsuffering.

Just like me with Buttons, He needs to jerk the reins repeatedly to keep me focused on His purpose for me. The major difference is, He doesn't get discouraged after one hundred jerks. He doesn't cry in frustration when I won't listen to Him. His mercies are new every morning, and His love never fails. His investment in me is eternal. So, He's willing to wait until I finally get it, and obey His lead.

I'm not there yet. I still need more jerks on my reins than I'd like. You, too?

Let's not get discouraged that we aren't learning as quickly as we'd like. Instead, let's rejoice that God never gives up on us. And let's pray that we'll learn to obey better than Buttons.

Two Scoops & a Sprinkle

❖ God cannot bless us beyond our willingness to follow His lead.

❖ If our lives are painful, it may be because we've wandered off the path.

❖ We don't have to grunt and struggle in our own strength to obey more readily. The Lord is happy to help us, if we're courageous enough to ask, "Soften my heart, Lord."

The Christmas Wedding Hero

"Forget yourselves long enough to lend a helping hand"
(Philippians 2:4 The Message).

I mean. How can you top first graders singing "Away in a Manger" accented by lisps from missing teeth as a wedding prelude? No one noticed the ruby poinsettia sprays draped over the end of each pew, or the candelabra's reflection on stained glass windows. We were too busy peering around heads to catch those six-year-olds singing. And singing. And singing.

After the third round of "Silver Bells," even the grandparents in the crowd started suspecting a glitch.

The bride's mother stilled our curiosity when she stepped to the front. "Is there an organist in the house?" she half shouted, half laughed. "Our organist is lost in Casey, and can't be here for forty-five minutes. If you can play, please step into the pastor's office to the left of the sanctuary."

Gasps and nervous chuckles shot through the crowd. But I knew someone who could save the day. "Honey, you can play," I whispered to my husband. "Go tell them you'll help."

"Oh, Jeanette, I don't play the organ—only the piano. It's a different instrument altogether. Surely in a crowd of this size, there's someone who's trained on the organ."

Not to betray my German heritage, I persisted. "No one is moving, Kev. You can do this. I know you can. Just don't use the foot pedals, and they'll never notice."

His eyes skimmed the room with a nervous gaze. "No, I don't think I could." He crossed his legs and pretended to find the wedding service bulletin interesting reading.

But no one else moved. And I don't give up that easily.

"Yes, you can. Now just go do it." My elbow may have slipped into his ribs; I don't remember.

With one final, desperate look around the room, Kevin rose from his seat. He moseyed to the door of the pastor's study, eyes on the carpet like a man going to the guillotine. As he pulled the door shut behind him, I sighed in relief. *Thank you, Jesus.*

Five minutes later, when he took his seat on the organ bench, a collective smile embraced all 200 guests. He played the processional like the first snowfall, sprinkling each bridesmaid with music as they glided down the aisle. He gained more confidence for "The Wedding March," and the bride received a full-scale storm of Wagner. By the recessional, organ music avalanched from his fingers. As the ushers dismissed each row, he bounced on the organ seat like a kid on a toboggan, playing original compositions, carols, and classical pieces.

No need for stairs from the platform to the sanctuary floor. Kev floated down and out to the sidewalk, his halo glimmering in the afternoon sun. His smile melted the snow as we walked to the car.

At the reception, guests lined up to congratulate the wedding superhero. He grinned and nodded between bites of cake, "I was happy to help"; "It was the least I could do"; and my personal favorite, "No problem at all!" I finally snatched his wallet and held up his driver's license next to his face.

"What are you doing, Jeanette?"

"Checking to see if I came with the right man."

He grabbed the wallet and stuffed it back into his pocket. "I just didn't want to steal the moment from anyone else who could play. Everyone might think I was showing off."

"No way would they think that about you, hon. Everyone could see you only wanted to help some friends out of a jam." I jabbed him in the ribs one last time, and straightened his halo.

Two Scoops & a Sprinkle

❖ Once we get past that first uncomfortable step, we often enjoy doing something we thought would mortify us.

❖ A little musical talent covers a multitude of silence.

❖ Sometimes it's okay to push a loved one into helping out, if you believe in their gifts, and they only need a wee nudge to step out and use a talent.

My Un-favorite Characters

"I can do all things through Him who strengthens me"
(Philippians 4:13 NASB).

We all have favorite characters—people we love to love because they make us better at being ourselves. But what about those who prick and poke us in all the wrong places, those un-favorite characters we'd rather live without? I restrained myself and narrowed my list down to the top six stinkers over the last three and a half decades of ministry.

Nellie Nasty: When we first met Nellie, she was the epitome of sweetness. But when we didn't operate programs in the church *her way*, she changed her flavor, saying nasty things about us in a congregational meeting and behind our backs.

Theodore Thrifty: Ted was a friendly guy until it came to money. Unfortunately, he was the treasurer of a church pastored. In his opinion, money should be hidden in a cigar box in a dark corner of the bank vault for a future emergency, not benefit the church or its pastor now. We went without a raise for five years at this congregation.

Eldon Extravagant: The reverse of Theodore, deacon Eldon wanted the church to have the best money could buy. He forgot it was not his money. His lavish spending dug our little congregation right into a hole so huge that we, as youth pastors hired last, were forced to leave.

Belva, Boris, and Brie Bickerson: Three members of the same family who loved to argue about *everything*. The trouble was, even they could never agree. Our Wednesday night Bible studies turned into squabbles over who authored the book of Hebrews and how many sisters Jesus had. It was enough to douse any flame the Holy Spirit may have started in seeking hearts.

Thankfully, none of these individuals occupies the pews or boardroom of our current congregation. All of my un-favorite characters lined the halls of past churches.

At the time we fought with—ahem, ministered to—these unsaintly saints, I was tempted to pull a James and John routine, asking Jesus if we could call down fire on them and get them out of our way. I was convinced we could do more for His kingdom without these human thorns in our sides.

In hindsight, however, I must confess that I'm grateful for the un-favorite characters who vexed us along the way. *Are you crazy?* you might be thinking. Well, yes, but that's another book. My reason to thank God for these prickly personalities is simple. Dealing with them helped me grow up.

Our job is people. Teaching, praying with, listening to, and loving people. As you have no doubt discovered, people are imperfect. Very few have sterling qualities that outshine the ugly traits. Most resemble me: I do my best to cover up my smelly side with the sweet perfume of grace, hoping you won't judge me too harshly when you discover a stinky fault.

Occasionally, we encounter someone who doesn't give a dirt clod what you think of them or who they hurt. These people afford us the opportunity to grow. Before you throw this book in the dumpster, let me explain.

How could I have learned to trust God for lies to be revealed and truth to win out if not for people like Nellie?

Experiences with both Ted and Eldon helped us to trust the Lord for finances rather than looking to our paycheck.

By their focus on the trivial, the Bickersons revealed to us what's truly important in the kingdom—loving God and His people.

I never relish clashing with someone who makes my life miserable. But I will always thank the Lord for the opportunity to develop a deeper walk with Him.

Two Scoops & a Sprinkle

❖ Rarely do we understand the value in a trial until it's over and we look back, viewing the Lord's provision and grace that brought us through.

❖ When I'm tempted to ask God to remove a thorn from our sides, He reminds me to pray for them instead. Something poking their souls causes them to act thorny. I may be the only one praying for them.

❖ Jesus handled each difficult person in His life in a unique way. As we seek God, He will show us how to relate to people in ways that bring honor to Him.

The Surprising Yellow Smile

"'Do not grieve, for the joy of the Lord is your strength'"
(Nehemiah 8:10 NIV).

Mom had major issues with my smile. From the time I was five or six, I heard her say, "I wish your teeth weren't so yellow. I don't know what caused that, but it sure bothers me." She even asked the dentist why my teeth were so dingy. Since teeth whiteners hadn't been invented yet, there was nothing the dentist could do to brighten my smile. Mom would just have to live with it.

I didn't mind. I still don't. I figure joy is color blind, and wants to express itself. So I smile anyway. It makes me feel yummy, like a bowl of chocolate raspberry ice cream, a purple balloon, a jiggle-bellied puppy, or a birthday present with a huge bow.

What if I had let Mom's embarrassment inhibit me? I might've quit smiling, thinking people would notice my yellow teeth and be horrified by them. Or I may have worried that my friends at school would make fun of me behind my back. Either way, I'd have missed a thousand blessings.

And so would the many people who've told me they loved my smile, how it made them feel comfortable in a roomful of strangers, or welcome in a new church. This yellow smile is a gift from the Lord, and I'm happy to share it.

I wonder how many gifts you and I have hidden or squelched because we didn't have the courage to say, "I like this about myself, and you are not stealing it from me just because it doesn't suit you." Sometimes we care too much what others think about us. We allow their opinions to shape our lives in ways the Master who created us never intended.

I don't mean we should be rude or defy authority. But we cheat ourselves, our society, and the world when we allow others to dictate how we act, based on their standards, rather than the Lord's individual plan for us.

Do you suppose people tried to tell Picasso he couldn't paint? Did they attempt to discourage Susan Boyle from a singing career? How many times did Abraham Lincoln have to ignore those who said he'd never succeed as a leader? Did C.S. Lewis throw his manuscripts away when more than eighty publishers rejected them?

Are you glad Pablo, Susan, Abe, and Mr. Lewis didn't listen to the doubters? Our world would be poorer and darker if they'd allowed the negative voices and opinions to shape their futures. But they didn't.

And you and I mustn't either. Even if our mother, our teacher, or our best friends aren't on board with our dreams, we must believe in our God-given abilities enough to stand strong in the face of opposition. Because we have the Mighty One living inside of us, we can be strong.

So go ahead and smile, even if it's yellow. Your colorful smile may give someone the hope he or she needs to live and breathe one more day. Sing your songs, make your speeches, paint your paintings, write your books, and build your dreams. The ones who tried to discourage you yesterday may be the very ones who benefit from your gifts tomorrow. Like my Mom.

She's long over disliking the yellow tint of my smile. Nowadays, she's just happy to have a daughter who loves and prays for her. And that makes me glad I kept smiling.

Two Scoops & a Sprinkle

❖ An indomitable spirit trumps a thousand naysayers.

❖ Since God is the giver of all good gifts, be pleased with the ones He gave you, even if others don't understand them. He put them in you because He knew you'd go places with them.

❖ Jesus' own brothers and sisters thought He was crazy. That didn't stop Him from following His heart and God's will. I imagine they all changed their mind when they saw Him resurrected.

Drive-by Diapers

"Does God give you his Spirit and work miracles among you because you observe the law, or because you believe what you heard?"
(Galatians 3:5 NIV).

I am so behind the times. My daughter in Tulsa, a mother of three, tells me about the new stores called Drive-by Diapers. In the middle of the night, or on the way to daycare, parents can purchase Junior's disposable drawers without leaving their car. The stores even provide menus displaying styles, sizes, and price ranges. My imagination soars with possible cross sales: "Would you like a tube of Desitin® with that?" or, "Need any pacifiers today?" Do you think the management supplies the gum-popping teens who staff the windows with 3 x 5 cards to stuff into the bags, offering tips for parents of babies with colic or fussy appetites?

I wonder what other drive-by ventures will emerge in the next few years. . . .

- *Night Crawlers Now*, for serious fishermen who can't wait till the bait shop opens
- *Hurry-up Hosiery*, for women prone to runs in the middle of the workday
- *Instant Ink Cartridges*, for those who run out while printing a legal document
- *Meal in a Minute*, for late-to-work breakfasters. You roll down your window; they throw the food into your mouth with one hand and scan your debit card with the other
- *Pronto Presents*, for frazzled birthday party shoppers. "Bob the Builder® gift wrap or Princess on Parade, ma'am?"

We shouldn't be surprised. Clinics zap patients with drive-by flu shots. Wedding chapels host drive-by weddings, where wannabe bouquet catchers sit in the backseat. Pharmacies boast speedy prescription refills at their drive-by windows.

Our society craves simple conveniences, which allow more time to focus on spouses, kids, and friends. We want to use our best days and hours on relationships, rather than tasks. That's a

God thing, really.

The Lord devised a simple, perfect arrangement to purchase us back from Satan and give us a place in His family. He sent Jesus to take on our guilt, die in our place, and provide us the gift of eternal, abundant life. His uncomplicated plan puts the savviest marketer to shame, because it focuses our attention on a relationship—with the One who gave His life for ours.

Our only task is to say yes to the gift that Someone Else paid for. It's as simple as driving to the pharmacy window to claim a prescription already charged to a loved one's Master Card. There isn't a way to earn God's love, favor, and kindness; we simply accept it. If God required us to pay for salvation, it wouldn't be a gift.

Some misunderstand the Lord's gift, and strive to earn the approval and love He's already purchased. They think their works will assure them a spot in heaven.

But when a person fully accepts what Jesus paid for, their outlook will change. Having become what the Bible calls "a new creature," they want to honor God from a heart of gratitude, rather than a need to pile good deeds into their heavenly shopping cart.

Have you discovered the simplicity of trusting the Lord to make you right with Him? If not, drive on up for a super-sized helping of grace and mercy. God is waiting for you at the second window. The best part is, it's already been paid for!

Two Scoops & a Sprinkle

❖ Refusal to accept God's grace is not only unbelief; it's pride. What makes us think we can earn God's love any more than the countless generations of people before us could?

❖ Modern innovations save precious time. But we mustn't let their convenience spoil us and tempt us to become impatient.

❖ The same simple faith in God's favor that brought us into His kingdom will help us live for Him. What we do for Him is a reflection of our gratitude, not a way to earn His love.

Let My Conscience Be Your Guide

"The Lord will continually guide you"
(Isaiah 58:11 NASB).

Why do some people consider it their duty to dole out unsolicited counsel to those in leadership? If the leader is new, the number of those in the Free Advice Club multiplies. They invite their friends to have a go, coaching them in the fine art of hinting, offering bright ideas and constructive criticism.

Christians love to help. Making suggestions on how to manage everything from money to marriage, and babies to breakfast food, is our way of giving the Holy Spirit a hand.

In one of our earliest congregations, we had an elderly lady I'll call Pieta who loved to buttonhole Kevin after Sunday worship, blessing him with her gift of criticism.

"We know you're trying to help us be friendlier, but we don't like the greeting time you've added to the church service. We're used to sitting down after we sing the opening song, not traipsing all over the auditorium shaking hands. It has to stop. *Everyone is upset about it.*"

"How many people have shared their concern with you, Pieta?" Kevin said.

She stopped to think. "Well . . . me and Josie Barnett."

Uncharacteristic of Kevin's peace-making nature, he boldly asked, "Just two of you are upset about this, out of the whole congregation?"

Pieta glared at him a moment, then huffed away, planning her next reproach-a-thon.

Not all the advice we've received in our many years of ministry has been critical like Pieta's. Some we found amusing or contradictory, like the following:

- When you preach, make it fun. Use more illustrations and visual aids.
- When you preach, don't use so many illustrations. Just read from the Bible, and let us draw our own conclusions.
- Let me teach you how to trim your beard and moustache with these two pages of detailed instructions (that one was for Kevin).
- This is how to buy a car, what kind of car to buy, and why you should buy my neighbor's car (which turned out to be a lemon).
- When you preach, don't stand behind the pulpit like a statue. Move about all over the stage and congregation. Put some energy into it!

- When you preach, just stay in one place. Don't move around or come down into the congregation.
- You need to talk less during the song service. Just lead the songs, nothing more. (Guess who this one was aimed at?)
- We love all the things you say when you lead songs. We want to hear more.
- You should not name your daughter *Esther*, but *Kevina*, after her daddy (thank God we had the presence of mind to reject that little nugget).

Because everyone has different expectations of how ministry leaders should look, talk, and behave, we will be juggling fiery brands if we try to act on everyone's advice. Worse than that, we will be following people's opinions instead of the Holy Spirit's leading.

Yes, we need to stay sensitive to the needs of those we minister to, not brutally careening over their feelings. Catering to individual preferences is another matter, however.

How do we learn to discern which ideas are keepers and which should be thrown back? The best way is to meditate often in God's Word, soaking up His grace and love. Then we pray long enough to hear His voice, and we obey what we believe He shows us.

Jesus loves Pieta as much as He loves us. She and her entire Take My Advice Club are precious to Him. But He isn't interested in what they think we should do regarding fellowship time in church. He wants us seeking His will and following it.

We'll enjoy our ministries and have happier congregations if He's the one we aim to please.

Two Scoops & a Sprinkle

❖ Confusion is a tool of the devil to keep us from listening to the Lord. If you are confused, ask a trusted friend to pray with you for clarity of mind. Then read God's Word until peace comes.

❖ If you aren't sure what direction to take on a certain matter, wait until you know. It's easier to play catch up than clean up.

❖ Don't disregard advice simply because you didn't ask for it. God may be speaking through a Pieta. Keep a humble heart, and have as much sense as a cow: learn to spit out the stubble and keep the hay.

I Don't Care What
Boo-Boo Thinks

"'Do not fear; let your hands be strong'"
(Zechariah 8:13 NASB).

Because I lean a bit toward people pleasing (*wait a minute, who am I kidding? I came out of the womb wearing an apron and holding an order pad, saying, "How may I help you?"*), I have often struggled with the sting and crush of unkind words.

"You were naughty today," Deidre said as she poked two-year-old Esther in the chest on her way out of church, and then turned to give me a caustic glare. I excused myself from the receiving line and dashed to the fellowship hall to wash communion dishes, leaving Estie with her daddy.

"I can't win," I sobbed to the Lord, my chest heaving with anger, tears spilling into the dishwater. "Last week Deidre told me I shouldn't take Esther out of the service every time she cried, that I should show her who's boss. So I kept her in today in spite of her crying, and Deidre pokes and scolds her. If I wasn't the preacher's wife, no one would dream of poking my baby!" A fresh spate of tears rained down as I grieved over the injustice. But I was just as angry at myself for trying too hard to please anyone who voiced an opinion over how I should do things.

Why is "the fear of men" so dangerous that the writer of Proverbs calls it a trap?

- When our goal is to please people, we give them a false sense of importance. We honor them with the admiration that is due to God alone. He calls us to live at peace with others, encourage, and bless them. But making sure everyone stays happy is not our job. It's their own.

- Everyone wants something different. How can we satisfy Art who thinks we should only use hymnals *and* Crystal who wants full-color PowerPoint slides for worship? How can we please them both? We can't.

- Enough is never enough. Faultfinders will create issues to pick over, because they enjoy the feeling of power it gives them. The more you go out of your way to make them happy, the more they are convinced they are right in their judgments. Then the more fault they will find. Their demands are like a fire that's never quenched.

What could I have done differently to show kindness and respect to Deidre without giving up my individuality? I could have politely thanked her for her input, then gone home and prayed about *God's* idea of how I should mother my children. Searching the Scriptures and finding ways to apply passages regarding children would've been a better use of my time and energy than jumping through all the hoops Deidre held out for me.

To embrace the personality God gave me, regardless of what others think I should be, grates against my deep need for approval and acceptance. But as I grow comfortable with the real me, I stand up on the inside, not needing the applause of humans to give me value.

The Lord's opinion of us is the only one that matters. As we search the Scriptures, we discover His deep commitment to us. Again and again, we see His plan of love and grace. When we choose to believe that love, we'll be set free to follow the unique plan He has for our lives. We break out of the prison of people-pleasing. We find our joy and fulfillment in God and God alone.

Do I care what Boo-Boo—my generic word for anyone-- thinks? Yes. Sometimes too much. But what my Father thinks overrides Boo-Boo's opinion every time.

Two Scoops & a Sprinkle

❖ When raising my children, I became so confused with the mountain of conflicting advice that I finally had to say, "Lord, you teach me how to do this." I learned my best child-rearing lessons in prayer.

❖ If you, like me, are programmed to please, it may help to peruse the New Testament epistles. Find each time the phrase "in Him" or "in whom" is used. These verses show us who we are in Christ and what God thinks of us. They build confidence in our hearts about our worth and value apart from others' estimation of us.

❖ Because God knows our hearts and motives, He is never shocked or disappointed in us. People may be upset when we don't act the way they think we should. But they are not God.

NO Is Not a Four-letter Word

"'But let your 'Yes' be 'Yes,' and your 'No,' 'No.' For whatever
is more than these is from the evil one'"
(Matthew 5:37 NKJV).

"Oh, boogers. I thought I made it clear that I didn't want to be an officer of the Missionary Mamas again. Now they've gone and nominated me for secretary. Dawn says no one else is willing to take it. What should I do, Kev?"

"Just say no, Jeanette. They know you are writing two books, working a full-time job, teaching a Sunday school class, and leading worship. Plus, feeding our houseful of cats takes up the rest of your spare time." He ducked as I threw a pillow at him. "They'll understand. And if they don't, oh well. You can't be all things to all women."

"But what if no one else will take the office?" I whined.

"You are not responsible for filling the offices for the Missionary Mamas, honey. And if they aren't filled, maybe it's time to end that ministry. Perhaps its mission is fulfilled."

I trudged to the phone to call Dawn, knowing I was going to disappoint her. My chest felt heavier than a pan of burnt biscuits. Yet I needed to let God lead me, not the needs and desires of others.

Kevin was right. She did understand. Two days later, they'd found someone else willing to serve.

Shortly after this, my friend Colette called, asking me to join her in a business project. I said yes immediately, only later stopping to pray and consider the venture from practical angles. I woke up several times during the night, debating with myself on both sides of the issue. After much prayer and counsel from trusted friends, I concluded the Lord wasn't leading me to partner with Colette. But now I worried that she'd be hurt if I backed out. What if it ruined our friendship? Finally, near the end of the day, I e-mailed her, letting her down as gently as I could. She surprised me by supporting my decision. Whew. All that fretting for nothing.

I have never had an easy time saying no. Yes is such a pleasant word, a fun word to say. It's the word autumn leaves make when they dance before the Lord in the afternoon sun. It's what you tell the minister on your wedding day when he says, "Do you take . . . ?" Doesn't it make everyone happy when you say yes?

No.

I had to learn that saying yes when I needed or wanted to say no was an excuse for not setting boundaries. With my kids when they wanted to stay up too late or watch too much TV. With my students when they treated me disrespectfully. And with those we pastored when they wanted me to lead vacation Bible school, write newspaper ads for the fall revival, and sing solos every Sunday.

None of those requests are wrong. But if I say yes to them to please people, I am leaving God out of the equation. I fail to fulfill the role He has mapped out for me. And I am hindering whomever He has called to do those things.

When I have the courage to set healthy boundaries, I enjoy the things God has told me to say yes to. I give others the opportunity to grow in their areas of expertise and develop courage to try new things they weren't brave enough to try before, because "Jeanette always does that."

I may not be as popular as I was in my yes days. But my heart sings with the freedom that results from saying no.

Two Scoops & a Sprinkle

❖ Saying no isn't only for setting boundaries with others. To stay free in the Lord, I must learn to say no to my fleshly desires. If I want to spend more money than I should, gossip, or lose my temper, I've learned that no is the safest place I can go.

❖ When we follow the leading of the Holy Spirit and are willing to say no, we won't burn out. We'll glow with God's peace.

❖ When God calls us to do a task, He gives the grace to accomplish it. If we're overwhelmed, we've added items that He never asked us to add. As we seek Him, He will show us what to eliminate, so we can be free from the tyranny of too much.

I've Fallen Off the Pedestal and I Refuse to Climb Back Up

"'For who is greater, the one who reclines at the table or the one who serves? Is it not the one who reclines at the table? But I am among you as the one who serves'"
(Luke 22:27 NASB).

This is one reason I sometimes wish people didn't know me as a pastor's wife, I grumped to myself. My friend Kirsten had told me I'd fallen off the pedestal she'd constructed for me. Seems she saw me jaywalking.

"Good," I said. "I didn't want to be up there anyway." A pedestal is a dangerous place to live.

Most of us reserve those glistening towers for people we admire. We hoist elected officials, sports champions, and entertainers upon them. This way our heroes can tower above the rest of humanity, like royalty looking down on the commoners.

Some ascend pedestals themselves. They enjoy the respect and attention, thinking it proves their significance. But when the crowds quit applauding and go home, the self-appointed idols try to sleep. Then they discover that marble makes an uncomfortable pillow. Pedestal-dwellers also don't get much company, because a huge ego ruins the best parties.

God placed into every heart a need to look up to and adore Him. We often try to fill that need with another person instead of God. This leads to trouble. Admiring someone too much sets us up for disappointment. When we aren't expecting it, they tumble down from their spire and crash at our feet. Whether it's jaywalking, losing their temper, or simply acting immature, something will cause the fall. No one can live up to others' unrealistic expectations of them. Life on a pedestal qualifies as unrealistic. Even for ministry leaders.

I imagine a few people like Kirsten have put me on a pedestal because I'm a minister's wife. I married a minister not because I aspired to be a hero, but because I fell in love with the man. To be candid, I have not enjoyed the limelight.

It gets in my eyes and keeps me from seeing Jesus.

I'd like to be who the Lord created me to be: an ordinary person like every one of His other children. Yes, God has called me to minister alongside my husband. Most of my ministry is to him. It's one of encouragement, prayer, laughing with him, and simply being his friend. I also teach Sunday school, write articles, speak, and sing. These are elements of my calling for which I claim no credit. I never fool myself that they make me better than those to whom I minister.

I can be a more enthusiastic cheerleader on the ground than in the sky where you can't see me. I can pray for you more effectively on my knees or sitting at my desk than on a cloud over your head. You will learn more from my life of transparency than you will if you paint a too-rosy picture of me.

Only one Leader deserves to be on a pedestal. I trust you know His name. He's the One who said, "If you want to be great in My kingdom, be a servant." Then He jumped down from the tower His followers had him on and washed their stinky feet.

That's my kind of hero.

Two Scoops & a Sprinkle

❖ I must pray to discern when another's need to have me as a role model has crossed over the line and become idol worship. I am learning to reject offers of ego elevating by keeping a humble attitude of servanthood.

❖ We can avoid Christian hero worship by refusing to hoist a favorite Bible teacher, musician, or author on a pedestal. It's okay to honor those we admire without placing them in a position of too much importance.

❖ The more time we spend worshipping the one true God, the less we are tempted to adore humans.

Tomorrow's Menu

"Don't fret or worry. Instead of worrying, pray. Let petitions and praises shape your worries into prayers, letting God know your concerns. Before you know it, a sense of God's wholeness, everything coming together for good, will come and settle you down" **(Philippians 4:6-7 The Message).**

As the nurse's aide entered our friend's hospital room, the first thing I noticed was the chartreuse silk flower on the end of her pen. *Wow, that's bright,* I thought. Then she smiled, and the flower's color dimmed to a dull green.

"Here's the lunch menu for tomorrow," she chirped. "Salisbury steak, baked potato, Viennese vegetables, banana pudding, and a yeast roll. What would you like to drink?"

"Wow, Viennese vegetables sound exotic," I said. "I've never heard of them."

"Oh, they're just mixed vegetables," said the aide, adding a chuckle. "It's a different blend each time, so the cooks give them an unusual name to make the meals sound appealing." She flipped through all the pages on her clipboard. "Tuesday we have Greek vegetables. Wednesday they serve Scandinavian vegetables. Thursday it's Polynesian. And Friday's feast includes Asian Delight." We laughed at the clever method of making the patients' stay a little more pleasant.

I have often wished God would allow me a glimpse of my future, even if I could only see tomorrow. Yet I understand why He doesn't. Knowing what was on tomorrow's menu for my life would either tempt me to fret and worry, or try to work out His plan in my own way.

If I knew Mom would call tomorrow and say, "We took your brother to the emergency room. They're keeping him overnight. His breathing is labored," I would probably not sleep too well tonight. Of course, I would pray for my brother, but I may not trust the Lord as much as I preach to others how they should not allow their hearts to be troubled.

If I knew I'd go out to the mailbox and find an unexpected check tomorrow, I'd have it spent before the mail carrier arrived. I may not even ask the Lord how He wanted me to spend and share it. Knowing ahead of time would tempt me to make a plethora of plans for the money—*my* plans for *my* money.

If I knew my son would text me tomorrow and say he's getting married, I'd have my mother-of-the-bride dress picked out, our flight reservations for the wedding trip booked, and his first two kids' names chosen before I even met his fiancée.

I'd best take one day at a time and follow Jesus' prayer of asking God to provide "our daily bread." Since God in His love and wisdom has not chosen to show us even the next moment's menu, He makes it simpler to trust Him.

I'm okay with that. I have learned—sometimes the rough way—that God loves me far more than I love myself, and His plan is always abundantly better than mine is. He has more ideas up His sleeve for blessing His kids than all the inventive minds of the centuries.

Like the brightness of that nurse's aide's smile compared to a faded silk flower, God's ways outshine our worst nightmares and best ideas. If we stick with today's menu, we'll live in His light and peace.

Two Scoops & a Sprinkle

❖ The writer of Hebrews tells us that without faith it's impossible to please God. Walking in faith usually requires not knowing the future.

❖ When we trust a person's character, we don't question their word, even if it seems far-fetched. Because God's character is love, we can trust His far-fetched promises to take care of us in all our tomorrows.

❖ Because I know that worry is a sin, I say, "I'm concerned." But it's all the same to God. I either trust Him, or not.

Time to Be God's Baby

"To whom He said, 'This is the rest with which you may cause the weary to rest,' and, 'This is the refreshing'; yet they would not hear"
(Isaiah 28:12 NKJV).

"Sit right here next to me and be my baby." Esther at age six was devoted to her younger brother, Ron. She'd recently learned to read, and wanted to share this talent with him. Patting the sofa beside her, she opened *Caps for Sale* on her lap.

But Ron whizzed down the hall, headed for the patio and his sandbox. As he raced past Estie, he hollered, "I don't have time to be your baby!" I laughed when I heard him, yet my heart ached for my daughter. She didn't need a chunk of Ron's time, just a smidgen, so she could show him she loved him. Ron had his own plans.

Do I treat God like this? I wonder. I rush to work, becoming impatient if I have to sit for two minutes at a red light. I zoom through my list of e-mails, ignoring the ones I think trivial, answering those I deem worthy of my time. I get mad at myself if I make a mistake I have to correct. Now I've wasted time. I dash through my tasks, even talking on the phone so quickly that customers ask me to repeat myself. I gulp down my lunch as I zip through as many blogs as I can squeeze into half an hour. Then I return to speed-work another four hours. When I arrive home, I hurry through supper so I can pinch in an hour of writing before I bustle into the shower, then finally plop into bed.

If there was a way to rush through my sleep, I'd discover that too. Then I could start tomorrow sooner, and accomplish more.

You'd think I was a *human doing*, rather than a *human being*. I rarely slow down long enough to relax and enjoy my relationship with God, to be His baby.

And while I run around getting high blood pressure, headaches, and acid reflux, God pats the spot next to Him on His throne and says, "Come sit here beside me and be my baby. I want to tell you how precious you are to me. I want to snuggle with you, and read my Book to you, and let you in on some secrets of mine. Be still a while, so I can love you."

Even if what I have planned seems more exciting than being at rest in His presence, I'd be a fool to reject His invitation. I'm always surprised what a little quiet will do for me. When I allow the Spirit of the Lord to love me in a way that no person or group of people will ever be able to, I am calmed, refreshed. My mind is cleared of confusion and worry. When I let His words of comfort from the Bible sink down deeply to bring healing in a way that no amount of meetings or parties could, my soul is renewed. He wants to pour some of His goodness into me, so my life will work right. Then I can tackle that schedule with more wisdom and strength than I dreamed possible.

Today, I won't disappoint the One who loves me the most. Today, I will slow down, and take the time to be God's baby.

Two Scoops & a Sprinkle

❖ Medical studies have shown that constant activity with no rest periods causes people to accomplish less than a combination of work—rest—work—rest. We are more productive when we add recreation and relaxation to our schedules.

❖ Listening to God can take many forms. For some, watching a sunset or sitting by a brook can open their hearts to the Lord's voice. Others hear Him through music or the spoken or written word.

❖ It took me more than fifty years to learn that the universe does not operate based on the amount of work I accomplish. Nor does it stop when I slow down a little to take some time off.

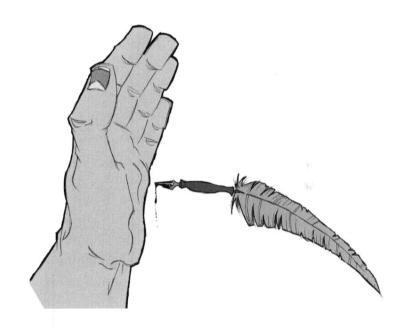

God's Tattoo

" 'He calls his own sheep by name and leads them out' "
(John 10:3 NIV).

When my friend Linda and I worked together, she became discombobulated over a computer procedure one day.

"Why the confused look?" I said. Her answer endeared her to me forever.

"Oh, I'm just trying to remember what I think I know."

I love her for saying that. She did it on purpose to make me feel better for my long history of ditzy doings. Like the day I sent my son to the store for "the liquid stuff you put on your cereal in the morning," because I couldn't think of the word for milk. Or the time I forgot to include flour in my cookie recipe for the Ladies' Aid Cookbook.

But my worst case of memory lapse was when I answered the phone several years ago in the midst of a stressful day and chirped, "Citizens Bank, this is . . ." I thought it was comical that I had forgotten my own name, but the customer on the other end was not amused.

Aren't you relieved God never forgets you? Before He spoke the stars into existence and commanded them to sing, He knew your name. Before He shaped the trees and bent the rainbow, He wrote your birthday on His calendar. Before you ever said yes to Him, He had reserved a place for you in the center of His heart.

The Lord has a unique way of remembering all His kids. Tattoos. If you don't believe me, look at Isaiah 49:15, 16 *NKJV*: "Can a woman forget her nursing child? And not have compassion on the son of her womb? Surely they may forget, yet I will not forget you. See, I have inscribed you on the palms of My hands." God is so in love with you, so thoughtful of your soul's deepest longings, that He's tattooed you on His hands.

"That's a pretty painful way to keep me in His mind," you may be saying. No more painful than nails in His hands and feet, holding Him to a cross meant for a criminal. Or a whip slicing His back at the hands of a merciless Roman soldier. And the brutal rejection of His own nation and family, who spat on Him and called Him crazy.

To Him, however, you are worth all the pain He endured to have you in His family and spend eternity with you. Jesus knew that the torture of His death and separation from His Father wouldn't last forever. But you will. So He willingly gave His life in your place.

If He'd go to such a painful death before your birth, how could He possibly forget you, now that you belong to Him?

When you have sacrificed your own comfort to give to someone in need, He does not forget your labor of love. When you have spent time in prayer for a person who's wronged you, He remembers your graciousness. When you long to tell someone off but keep your mouth shut, He notes your self-control. Every time you pass up a sin or repent of one, He remembers your obedience. When you are in trouble or anguish, He hears every cry and collects every tear.

Whether God has actually tattooed or simply written you on His hand, you are forever on His mind. Unlike Linda and me, He never forgets a name—*yours*.

Two Scoops & a Sprinkle

❖ When we're in the midst of a mess, we may feel like God has forgotten us, even though we know He's promised never to leave us. It's okay to ask Him to remind us of His love. He has a thousand creative ways to show us how much He cares.

❖ What made Jesus endure the torture of the cross and misunderstanding from his best friends? Nothing made Him. He chose to give His life, so we could be part of His family.

❖ Just as God has carved us on the palm of His hand, we need to carve His words into our hearts, so we won't forget Him.

Ditzy? Maybe. Stupid? Never!

"Therefore judge nothing before the appointed time; wait till the Lord comes. He will bring to light what is hidden in darkness and will expose the motives of men's hearts. At that time each will receive his praise from God"
(1 Corinthians 4:5 NIV).

I looked up the word "ditzy" in my dictionary. It's not there. It's not even in our enormous book of *Word and Phrase Origins*. Imagine that. But I think I can define it myself. "Distracted. Not thinking from cause to effect. Prone to irrational behavior. Illogical."

I'll give you a few examples.

When I was twelve, I fell off a skateboard and broke my arm. I had pushed off with the foot that was on the board instead of pushing off with the grounded foot. Oh, well. I had the thrill of a handsome doctor in the emergency room, and got all those signatures on my cast.

215

When my kids were little and I was rushing about, I sometimes called one by the other's name. They didn't seem to mind, but it embarrassed me. I only had two kids, and they were different genders.

In the lunchroom at my former job, I called the facilities manager to report that the battery on the wall clock needed replacing. He hurried down from his office on the third floor, pointed to the dangling cord, and dryly remarked, "Jeanette, I don't think so. This is an *electric* clock!"

Could I help it that I hadn't noticed the cord, which was the same color as the wall? I was looking at the *face* of the clock.

Ditzy? Maybe. Stupid? Never. I did find "stupid" in the dictionary, and it is scary. "Given to unintelligent decisions or acts; lacking reason; senseless" (Merriam Webster's Collegiate Dictionary, Tenth Edition). Are you wondering what the difference is? I'm SO glad you asked.

Ditzy is a person who is normally of sound mind occasionally doing something that doesn't make sense. Any number of factors can cause ditziness. You didn't get enough sleep last night because your cat wanted out 254 times; they are playing rap music on the radio, and you can't concentrate when that's on; your kid is sick, and you're worried about him; your spouse is mad at you; you are mad at your spouse; your best friend is going through a divorce; your daughter is about to have a baby; your mom is in the hospital. These kinds of things occur in all our lives. They throw us off balance, causing us to forget our names and what planet we reside on.

Stupid is another story. Stupid is a doctor who tells a woman she will never be a mother, and when she turns up pregnant, he guides her through nine months of wondrous fetal development, delivers that tiny miracle, and says, "There is no God." Stupid is a scientist who has a doctorate in astronomy, helps create and put in place the Hubble Space Telescope, teaches at a renowned college, and isn't sure if a Higher Being designed the universe, or it "banged" into existence one day.

Stupid is walking away from a friend who needs you. It's neglecting your spouse, child, or pet. It's not showing up to work, or leaving a good job just because someone offended you. It's not paying your bills; not saying, "I love you," to those who matter. It's being irresponsible, thoughtless, and rude.

Have you noticed that God counts intelligence in a different way than we do? He puts a high priority on compassion, honesty, diligence, and generosity. He doesn't care if you call your kids the wrong name or forget to put butter in the muffin recipe. He's just happy you are talking to the kids and cooking for your sick neighbor. It's okay with Him that you wore your slippers to church. He's just happy you showed up. It doesn't matter to Him that you call David "Daniel" or Sierra "Sarah." He thinks it's commendable that you're trying to honor someone by using his or her name.

He's interested in character. Not perfect performance. I'd say that makes Him smarter than all of us put together.

Two Scoops & a Sprinkle

❖ If we worry that we'll do or say something stupid or ditzy, we may never attempt anything.

❖ We can learn from our dumb mistakes as much as or more than we learn from our successes.

❖ Forgiving ourselves for errors and ditziness is a sign of maturity and self-confidence.

You Love Me

*"And you have forgotten that word of encouragement that
addresses you as sons: 'My son, do not make light of the Lord's
discipline, and do not lose heart when he rebukes you, because
the Lord disciplines those he loves, and he punishes everyone
he accepts as a son'"*
(Hebrews 12:5-6 NIV).

Her hug was no different than usual. Her tanned arms and spindly legs wrapped around my neck and waist like summer vines. It was her words that surprised me.

Four-year-old Jenessa had always said, "I love you" as sweet as grape jelly when she hugged Kevin or me, parroting the words we'd told her since she was born. They were the same words we'd spoken to our own two kids, words every child deserves to hear often. This time as she snuggled against my neck, she said in a calm, confident tone, "You love me."

"Yes, I do!" I laughed, embracing her tighter. I was pleased she felt secure enough not to ask me if I loved her, but to tell me. Was she reassuring herself, or reminding me?

Jenessa, along with her two-year-old brother, baby sister, mommy, and daddy had stayed with us for the week of vacation Bible school. Just as I'd done nearly thirty years earlier with her mama, I corrected her a *dozenty* times each day. "Don't tell me you want a banana. Ask, 'May I please have one?' "Swallow your food before you tell us something. We don't want *see food* at this table." "Sit still, honey. I can't read to you if you keep wiggling the book."

I'd also cuddled, kissed, and teased her. I played with her in the sandbox in the blistering heat. I bought her a new coloring book and crayons, and colored with her, comparing our favorite shades of purple. I watched endless episodes of Mr. Rogers' Neighborhood and read countless library books. I even shared my expensive frozen yogurt with her.

So she took my correction in stride, knowing that my love undergirded everything I said. She obeyed me—most of the time—and didn't pout when I scolded. Her young heart seemed to crave the many boundaries I set.

God corrects us too, sometimes more than we like. Perhaps He convicts us when we think poorly of someone, have a sour attitude, even when we're hard on ourselves. He's never harsh or unkind when His still, small voice whispers in our hearts to come up higher, so we can be happier. His boundaries are the security our hearts need.

Then there's His fun, loving side. He makes our tomato and zucchini plants grow into Jack's beanstalks so we can have the joy of sharing. He sends us people who make us laugh when we're facing a doctor's report, or lets us meet someone with a smaller home than we live in so we'll be thankful. He puts us in a family called a church so we don't have to bear our burdens in solitude. He gives us His Holy Spirit to comfort us. His Word to renew our hope. His blood to forgive us. All proof that His supreme love is what motivates everything He does, even correcting us.

What else can we do but climb into His lap and tell Him, "You love me!"

Two Scoops & a Sprinkle

❖ Love is the ideal balance of giving and boundaries, never overboard on one side or the other. God is the only example of perfect love—His corrections are never too harsh, His giving never too indulgent.

❖ The younger or more disobedient a child is, the more correction they need. This is true of believers as well. The more we obey the leading of the Holy Spirit, the less correction we require.

❖ If you find it easy to receive God's correction but not His gifts, you may need to spend more time in the New Testament Epistles such as Ephesians and Colossians, where the Lord shows us our privileges in Him.

Dings and Beeps

" 'Now fear the Lord and serve him with all faithfulness' "
(Joshua 24:14 NIV).

"What are those extra bells?" I asked as I buckled up. "I thought this car only chimed six times when you first got in, to remind you to put your seatbelt on. That was ten dings I heard just now."

"Oh, it's telling me that I need to change the oil," said Kev, as thrilled as I was for the extra noise every time we entered the car. "I'll take care of it this weekend."

A few weeks later, as we were on the way to shop, more extra dings. Only this time they waited until we were a few miles down the road. "What now?" I moaned.

Kevin pushed his glasses up his nose and squinted. "Oh, there's a blue light on the dash that we need to add windshield wiper fluid."

"Good grief! I suppose in the winter there'll be three more dings and an orange light to remind us to put our defroster on.

Then when the tires are low, we'll have a purple light and it'll ding us to put air in them, and so on. This is the naggingest car we've ever owned!"

Then there's our stove. You set the timer, and you get an obnoxious, high-pitched *beep-beep-beeeeeeeep* when it's done. *But that's not good enough*, the programmers thought. *We must beep those cooks five times in ten-second increments till they come and turn the timer off.* How thoughtful of them. I'll bet they never baked a casserole or a cookie in their lives.

We used to have one of those old-fashioned spring timers that only goes up to 60 minutes. You set it and it dings once. Treats you like an adult. If you don't get your clothes out of the dryer or your cookies out of the oven, tough. At least it lets you decide if you want to take care of something. It doesn't nag you to death until you do.

As a young adult, you are so thrilled when you finally grow up, leave home, and don't have Mom and Dad around all the time to remind you to do things like change the motor oil, use your seatbelt, and get the lasagna out of the oven. Now you can conquer life in your own way, create your own paths through the wilderness, find the unique blueprint for your life. Then the car, washing machine, and stove manufacturers come along and remind—nag—you, taking over for Mom and Dad.

Just in case you haven't learned to think for yourself. It's insulting.

Aren't you glad God isn't into nagging? He lets us decide what we are going to do with His Word, with His plan for us, with Jesus. A few dings and beeps here and there along the way let us know that we are making a wrong choice or disobeying Him, and we'd better turn around if we want a peaceful life. But He never nags. He leaves the choices up to us so that we learn to decide wisely. He trusts us.

Kind of scary, because the consequences of our choices are a lot more serious than dirty motor oil or burnt cookies. However, God knows what He is doing. If He didn't let us decide on our own to follow Jesus, all He'd have would be a lot of robots, worshipping Him because we had to. A bunch of programmed ding-dongs. Not much fun for either Him or us.

Love God because you choose to, because He offers you eternal and abundant life. Prove to Him and yourself that you have the brains to make great choices. Don't be a ding-dong.

Two Scoops & a Sprinkle

❖ Humans invented nagging as a method of influencing others. The Holy Spirit guides, comforts, encourages, convicts, and leads.

❖ If we ignore the Lord's voice long enough, our hearts may grow dull of hearing. The best way to keep a soft heart is to obey His gentle nudges. He always leads us in paths of blessing and light.

❖ Our free will must often break God's heart when we choose foolish ways. It's the freedom to choose that makes our relationship with Him sweet.

Be Somebody

"Jesus said to her, 'Daughter, you took a risk of faith, and now you're healed and whole. Live well, live blessed! Be healed of your plague'"
(Mark 5:34 The Message).

"Too many people," I moaned as Kevin and I turtled through the traffic in Portland, Oregon, on an Indian-summer afternoon. We sweated and sighed for more than an hour to travel twelve miles along a freeway clogged with commuters.

"I think living in rural Illinois has spoiled us," said Kev. "We've forgotten how crowded and hectic the city can be. How impersonal."

We may contend with millions instead of thousands, but the cities in Jesus' day were just as chaotic and unfriendly, especially when He was in town. The multitudes pushed and shoved to get a peek at Him or to touch His clothes. One little lady fought extra hard and long to make her way to Jesus.

The woman with a twelve-year-old hemorrhage in Mark 5 broke Jewish law to be out in public with her condition. Yet she risked people seeing and recognizing her to find Jesus and simply touch the hem of His garment. "If I do that, I know I'll be healed." Over and over, she repeated these words to herself. They alone gave her the strength and courage she needed to press through the crowded, sweaty streets and finally reach the only One who could help her.

"*Somebody* touched me. Who was it?" Jesus asked, stopping on His way to heal the daughter of a man named Jairus. Some may have snickered behind Jesus' back at what seemed like a silly question.

"Master, you see this vast crowd," said Peter. "Everyone here is jostling and shoving to make a path to you. How can you say, 'Who touched me?'"

"*Somebody* touched me," Jesus persisted, scanning the crowd in all directions. "I felt healing power leave me."

Trembling with fear, the woman spoke up, telling Jesus how she'd crawled through the dusty, pushy throng, knowing if she could only touch Jesus' hem, she'd be well.

Jesus did not rebuke her. He complimented her courage. "Go in peace, Daughter, and be healed of your plague. Your faith has made you whole," He said, His tender voice cancelling her fear.

Here was a nobody, a chronically sick woman who'd had no hope of recovery until she heard of Jesus. When she forced her way through the mob to touch a scrap of His clothing, like a mighty magnet her faith pulled God's healing power out of Him.

In that instant, she became a *somebody*. A special *somebody* whom Jesus took time to encourage. In that shining moment, He dignified her and lifted her beyond the physical healing she had hoped for.

The term "daughter" in Jesus' time and culture was akin to us calling a close friend or family member "sweetheart" or "dear." Jesus not only healed this broken woman, He personally named her *beloved*.

Jesus' words gave her significance and value. This woman was never the same from that moment forward, knowing she was precious to Him.

What plagues you today? Do you feel that you, like this woman, are a nobody? Has your problem lived with you so long, you despair of a solution? Please don't. Use what faith you have, no matter how small, to press through to Jesus. Keep saying to yourself, *I know He has what I need. I know I will be made whole when I touch Him. I am His beloved.*

Don't let the crowd of doubts and the mob of Satan's lies keep you from your miracle. Your faith will give you courage to touch Jesus. He has everything you need to make you whole. He will dignify you and turn you from a nobody to a *somebody*. You are His "sweetheart." Once you touch Him, you will never be the same again.

Two Scoops & a Sprinkle

❖ Jesus is not only interested in crowds of humanity, but each individual and his or her unique issues.

❖ If this little lady had followed the rules and traditions of her culture, she'd have missed her miracle.

❖ To the world, we may be a nobody. In Jesus' heart, we hold a special place no one else can fill.

Estie and Uncle Ken

"Do not withhold good from those who deserve it, when it is in your power to act. Do not say to your neighbor, 'Come back later; I'll give it tomorrow'—when you now have it with you" **(Proverbs 3:27-28 NIV).**

Kevin's Uncle Ken was a brilliant aerospace engineer. One of the last projects he worked on before retiring was inventing ways to keep the tiles on the early space shuttles from dislodging during reentry. He must've had a thousand fascinating stories to tell, if he would. But not Uncle Ken. Getting him to talk was like trying to get the magenta crayon out of the box with your eyes closed.

When the kids were young and Uncle Ken lived nearby, he'd pop in every few months. We'd smile a welcome, offer him a soda, and pray for the time to go quickly. Fortunately, I can talk to a filbert tree and find something we have in common—we're both nutty—but even I was challenged by the taciturn Uncle Ken.

It was not my idea of fun, but he was Kevin's uncle, he was a lonely bachelor, and we wanted to be kind. He wasn't a terrible fellow. He just didn't have much to say.

One afternoon, the uninformative Uncle Ken popped over during a stage in four-year-old Estie's life. Every time a visitor drove away after their visit, she'd stand at the door wailing, "But, I wanted to go with them!" As a typical four-year-old, she didn't want to miss any excitement.

Ken had no way of knowing the trauma he was about to cause our girl that day. The visit started out as always, with Uncle Ken plopping onto the sofa, Estie and Ron emerging from their room, saying "hi," and then deserting Kevin and me to spend the rest of the afternoon stretching our brains for conversation topics, silently praying for that magenta crayon.

At last, Uncle Ken stood up to leave. He poked his head into the kids' room for a quick "'bye," then zipped out the door and down the street. Kevin and I looked at each other and sighed with relief. Suddenly, it began raining buckets from Estie.

"But, I wanted to go with him!" She sobbed her remorse over another missed opportunity. By an act of God, we managed to hold back our laughter while we comforted her, wondering at the ridiculous notion of Uncle Ken entertaining a preschooler for more than thirty seconds.

And thirty years later, we remember that scene and think, *We rarely appreciate someone until after they leave.*

It's human nature to take people for granted, especially ones we've lived with or known for years. Their tacky little habits irritate us. They don't do things our way. They talk too much or not enough. They hurt us without meaning to, but it's still painful.

If they should leave for a week or a month or permanently, we realize we liked having them around. Their annoyances don't seem to loom as big as their absence. We may not sob as Estie did, but our regret is just as real. We missed opportunities we'll not have again, and that load weighs heavy on our hearts.

Before you reach for your hankie, I have some good news. *It doesn't have to stay this way.* If you have one breath left, you can start today to show the significant people in your life that you love and appreciate them.

It's okay to say, "I'm glad you're my friend. You have helped me become a better person." It's okay to hold your spouse's hand and look into their eyes and tell them, "I'm happy I married you," or say to your kids, "You are a gift. You're gonna make it."

What you have with you is today. Use it to let the people who mean the most to you know how you feel about them. While they are still here, make sure they know you're glad they are here.

Two Scoops & a Sprinkle

❖ As uncomfortable as it is to say, "forgive me," it's worse to wish you could say it and not be able to.

❖ Taking time to show appreciation today is an investment in the future, both yours and the person you appreciate.

❖ Although you might find it easier to give corrections than compliments, developing the habit of encouragement will increase your list of loyal friends.

Minor Alterations

"'Have I not commanded you? Be strong and courageous. Do not be terrified; do not be discouraged, for the Lord your God will be with you wherever you go'"
(Joshua 1:9 NIV).

Mom loves to mend so much, she once took a robe with a broken zipper home in her suitcase, fixed it, and mailed it back to me. I wouldn't dare say aloud that I think this borders on radical, because she might stop mending my clothes, and then where would I be?

I did not inherit that particular gene. I will pin stray buttons and tape loose hems in place just to avoid getting out my needle and thread or my sewing machine. Minor alterations seem like chores to me. I would rather sew an entire garment than mend one.

But when it comes to life, minor alterations can make a major difference in getting a job done, relating to a person, or changing an attitude. For instance . . .

It takes me about thirty seconds to choose tomorrow's outfit tonight, but five minutes if I do it in the morning when I'm fuzzy-brained. That's four and a half more minutes I can spend drinking caffeine!

I feel like I should minister more to a friend who doesn't know the Lord. I can preach to them every time I see them, possibly scaring them off. Or I can start praying for them whenever I pass their house, asking God for practical opportunities to share His love.

If I am brief when I have an idea to tell my husband, planting a little seed instead of sowing the entire field for half an hour, he receives it more readily. It doesn't mean he's always going to do what I want. It means that peace reigns in our home. I am learning the beauty of conciseness.

I need to spend extra time with the Lord, so He'll be more real to me than the problems I face. If I get up an hour earlier every day to pray, I will soon burn out and quit. If I add just five minutes in the morning and five at night talking to Him, or turn off the TV and replace it with Christian music, I can live with that minor alteration. The peace of mind it brings is refreshing.

When we see things in our lives that require change, we may panic. We mistakenly believe only a major overhaul will bring about the change, get discouraged, and never try. Our circumstances remain the same—or get worse.

Be encouraged, my friend. Minor alterations can and do make huge differences. Don't let Satan lie to you, telling you that your situation will never change, or that it will take too much work to change it, like sewing a garment from scratch rather than mending one. Listen to God. He says, "Do not be afraid or dismayed. I am with you wherever you go." The Holy Spirit is in us to be our helper. He will not let us down. Whatever minor alterations we need to make, He will help us. Victory is ours, if we'll ask Him what to do.

Perhaps I should practice what I'm preaching. A pair of pants with the hem out has been calling to me. . . .

Two Scoops & a Sprinkle

❖ Satan would like to convince us that we must finish every chore at one sitting, so we'll get discouraged and never start. If we break tasks down into baby steps, they become manageable.

❖ We often fear change because of "uns"—change makes us uncomfortable, and the outcome is unknown. If we'll let Him, God will take our fears and give us faith. Then we'll be ready to make some minor alterations.

❖ Small adjustments shine their brightest in relationships. A little more listening here, a bit more understanding there, lead to remarkable growth and harmony.

Sticks, Stones, and Words that Wound

"I can do all things through Him who strengthens me"
(Philippians 4:13 NASB).

Gerry's words drew blood from my heart like re-stubbing a toe. After he'd rebuked me in front of friends at church, I felt like running the three miles home and never returning.

Hiding my wounds throughout the service, I swallowed the sobs in my throat. I felt like a liar as I sang, "The Joy of the Lord" when my heart lay weak and wounded. But when we got home, I knew I had to get alone and pray.

"Dear Lord, I forgive and bless Gerry for his unkind words to me today. I bless his family, his health, his finances—"

"Whoa there, Jeanette. You can't just shove your hurt under the mobile home like that."

"But, Lord, you said to bless and pray for those who wrong me."

"Yes, I did. But you need to deal with the wrong first, and get it out in the open. Tell me about it."

Startled by this foreign idea, I began, my voice soft and halting. "Well, Gerry was rude to me, Lord."

"Yes."

A little bolder, "He was mean. Even if he needed to correct me, he should have done it in private. It was insensitive of him to scold me right before worship, in the center aisle for everyone around to hear!" My voice held a chord of confidence now as I strode around the bedroom. I could feel the tension releasing its grip on my shoulders.

"Yes, I know. Anything else?"

"No, I guess not." I sniffled, walking to the dresser for a tissue. I wondered what was next.

"I agree with you, Jeanette. Gerry should not have said those things to you, especially in front of your friends. He was rude and unkind."

I blew my nose and listened.

As He continued, His gentle voice caressed my heart. "Let me ask you, Daughter. Have you ever hurt someone, or embarrassed them in front of others?"

"Oh yes, Lord. Tons of times. I even caused a girl to get fired at a job, because I griped so much to the boss about her. I still cringe when I remember that, Lord."

"And did I forgive you for that, as well as all the other times you've behaved horribly?"

I gulped. "Well, of course. You always forgive me."

"Do you think you can reach down into your soul, and extend a bit of the grace I've poured into you, to Gerry? Can you, in spite of how he wronged you, allow him to go free of having to make it up to you? Can you release him into My hands, to deal with him in My way?"

"Well, yes, when you put it that way, Lord, I can." I took a deep breath. "Okay, Lord, here goes. I choose to forgive Gerry, even though he treated me like poop. You have freely forgiven me for every wrong I've ever committed, many of them worse than Gerry's meanness. So, I extend the grace you've put into my heart, to him. Please help him, Lord. Let him feel your love . . ."

Now I could freely pray for Gerry and bless him without rancor. I won't say the hurt left immediately, but it subsided and eventually scooted out as I continued to pass along the Lord's grace to my brother. Then the very peace of God, like a yummy orange sunset washing over the horizon, soothed my wounded heart.

Yes, words injure far worse than sticks and stones. But Jesus' love extended to us and through us can heal the deepest wounds of our souls.

Two Scoops & a Sprinkle

❖ It's okay to tell the Lord about your hurt and anger over a wrong. Pretending you aren't hurt won't solve the problem. Get it out in the open, allowing Him to pour His love into your wounds.

❖ When fellow Christians sin against us, we never feel like forgiving them. A good first step is to say, "Lord, I'm not willing to forgive this person just yet. But I am willing for you to help me become willing."

❖ Even Jesus got His feelings hurt. But He didn't wallow in the pain. He extended His Father's grace to His tormentors and stayed free of bitterness.

Culture Shock

"Where can I go from your Spirit? Where can I flee from your presence? If I go up to the heavens, you are there; if I make my bed in the depths, you are there"
(Psalm 139:7-8 NIV).

As our plane touched down at the Indianapolis airport, my eyes spilled with grateful tears. God had given us our hearts' desire: to trade the swarming city life for the serene, caring community of rural Paris, Illinois. He'd fulfilled our ten-year- long dream of moving to the Midwest.

My elation lasted a whole two weeks.

After our dishes, books, and cat toys were unpacked, the newness of our peaceful environment faded. Although surrounded by friendly faces and caring hearts, we were lonely. You can't replace in a few weeks friendships you've built over fifteen years. And the winding country lanes presented more of a challenge to us than the freeways of L.A.

243

Just when I was ready to pack my cat carriers and point my car west, God did it. He brought some special, caring people into our lonely corner of the world who knew what we needed and took the time to share it.

One evening shortly after we arrived in Paris, Grace pulled into our driveway. "Hop in," she said, handing Kevin the keys. She took the back seat, and gave me a pad and pencil. Grace knew the best way for us to learn the streets of our new hometown was to drive them ourselves. Following her helpful instructions, I drew a map of all the major streets, noting businesses, hospitals, and restaurants.

A lovely widow, Faith, invited us to share our first Thanksgiving, Christmas, and Easter with her and her kids. Knowing we were two thousand miles from our family, she made us feel like members of hers. Faith also appointed herself captain of Kevin's cheerleading squad, continually telling him what a great preacher he was.

One of our elders, Don, discovered that eating out was my favorite sport. This generous man treated us to Sunday dinner for a year. He also took up offerings our first few Christmases here, buying new furniture and a freezer for our home.

Patty and Del helped us find a new car, repaired our garage door, and filled our new freezer with beef from theirs. They took the prize for generosity when they gave us a lovely hutch they'd purchased at an estate sale, claiming it didn't fit in their dining room. Only the Lord knew I'd wanted a hutch for decades, but hadn't the money to buy one.

I call these kinds of sweet gestures "hugs and kisses from God."

We are ready to abandon something God called us to do, and He sends someone to say, "I appreciate your work." We wonder if we're wasting our time and talent throwing pearls to ingrates, and He prompts somebody to tell us how we've made a positive difference in their life.

We long for the dining choices in the big city, and He nudges a generous couple to invite us out for ribs. At these times, I can hear the Father saying, "I've got you covered, Kids. I've not forgotten you. You're in a strange place, but you're still in the center of my heart."

It helps to remind ourselves that through every shock we face, God knows where we are, both geographically and emotionally. He has helpers everywhere who recognize the kind of encouragement we need, and He knows how to get them to us.

Let's not run away from new experiences too soon. Where we live today may not feel comfortable, but if we ask the Lord for a little help from some friends, we'll discover that wherever He lives, is home.

Two Scoops & a Sprinkle

❖ We need to allow ourselves time to recover from culture shock. We cannot duplicate the friendships or experiences from our former culture. However, if we take our cares to the Lord, He'll make the new experiences as rich and sweet as the old ones.

❖ People love to say, "You can't teach old dogs new tricks." I reply, "We are not dogs." Our challenge arises when we refuse to learn new ways, or don't give ourselves enough time to adjust to different surroundings.

❖ Embracing a new culture doesn't mean we must throw out all our past methods and thinking. We still don't eat biscuits and gravy, but we love the people who do.

Sharing My Messes

"Here is a trustworthy saying that deserves full acceptance:
Christ Jesus came into the world to save sinners—of whom I
am the worst. But for that very reason I was shown mercy so
that in me, the worst of sinners, Christ Jesus might display
his unlimited patience as an example for those who
would believe on him and receive eternal life"
(1 Timothy 1:15-16 NIV).

I opened my women's Sunday school class with a confession. "Am I the only one who isn't enjoying this study? When I look at the book title, *Me and My Big Mouth*, I want to throw it into the fireplace. I'd rather scrub my kitchen floor than discover that complaining is a sin. The first word out my mouth was a complaint that the delivery room was too cold. I could win a blue ribbon at the state fair for the most gripes in an hour."

Hope laughed her loudest. "That's why I love this class, Jeanette."

"Because your teacher has an awful time getting her tongue in order?"

"No. Because you're honest enough to admit it. We feel comfortable with you when you share how you struggle with the same issues we do."

They knew how impatient I became when customers at work had unreasonable requests; how I condemned myself when one of my kids made a poor choice; how I struggled to submit to my husband's leadership. And they loved me anyway. I like to think they loved me more than if I'd pretended I never took a wrong turn.

Before I became a pastor's wife, I wouldn't have dreamed that sharing my faults could make someone happy. Didn't people expect a leader to set a perfect example? Didn't they want the pastor's wife to show them how easy it was to walk in all the fruit of the Spirit? Didn't they need a model saint who never yelled at her kids or had a tacky thought? Maybe not.

I don't enjoy listening to speakers or reading authors who want to tell me how to get it right without revealing how they first got it wrong. Have a diet book? I won't read it if you've never been addicted to comfort food, or never had to lose more than ten pounds. Wanna tell me how to have a successful marriage? I refuse to listen if you're single or you've never been in a fight with your spouse. (Besides, I'd think you're lying.)

Battle scars are the best proof that I *can* trust you to lead me in a war. I know you understand my fears when you share your stories of how God helped you overcome yours. When you get on your knees to pray and cry with me out of empathy rather than pity, I will listen to any advice you give me.

Perhaps the women in my Sunday school class feel the same. They see that although I'm a leader, I stumble like they do. I face the same temptations and struggle with the same battles as everyone I lead. Yes, I share my victories and answers to prayers. But I'm quick to tell them that to be successful in this life they need to look to the Master. I'm not the one to copy. Anything in my life that's worthy of emulating was placed there by Jesus.

If my transparency can give people hope, I'm okay with sharing my messes. Because if God can take someone as messy as me and turn them into a leader, He can fix anyone.

Two Scoops & a Sprinkle

❖ Although it's important to be transparent with those you lead, people sometimes carry it too far. We need to be aware of how much honesty each of our friends can handle. If we share too much too soon with people, it may scare them. Always follow the leading of the Holy Spirit. If in doubt, don't.

❖ Laughing at ourselves is a great way to break free of taking our little lives too seriously.

❖ A friend who taught a Bible study in a women's prison once looked at all the gorgeously dressed ladies at a banquet. She remarked to me, "We all have the same problems inside. Some of us just dress them up fancier on the outside."

Farmer Girl

"So let's not allow ourselves to get fatigued doing good.
At the right time we will harvest a
good crop if we don't give up, or quit"
(Galatians 6:9 The Message).

"Are you going through culture shock yet?" asked Stan while he shook my hand on the way out of church. We had moved from Los Angeles to rural Illinois two weeks earlier. I wondered if my smile looked too pasted on, or I'd failed to put enough makeup on the circles under my eyes.

"Oh, no, we're fine. I do miss the salad bars in the restaurants in the city, though. I'd sure love to plant a garden. The only time I attempted one, it turned into a disaster. I read the instructions wrong on the onion seed package and planted them ten inches deep and two inches apart instead of the other way around. I think I'll need some help this time."

After wiping his eyes from laughing at my onion oops, Stan said, "Look no further. I'll be glad to help. Let's go take a look-see where you might have a good spot to plant. Then when the ground warms up a little, I'll bring my tiller over."

I arrived home from work one afternoon in late April to find my garden plot not only tilled but planted—Stan had outdone himself with onions, garlic, radishes, carrots, green beans, peppers, tomatoes, and corn. Throughout that spring and summer, he walked out to the garden plot with me each Sunday, patiently teaching me the finer points of gardening.

"Take your spade every few days and loosen the soil around these onions, so they can breathe and expand. Same with the carrots. They grow better if they aren't so tightly packed."

"Radishes need a lot of water or they'll taste too hot. If it hasn't rained in a few days, you may want to turn the sprinkler on them."

"Keep picking these peppers, and they'll produce for you all summer long."

I found growing vegetables more strenuous than I'd imagined, and developed great admiration for those who kept a garden every year. I hoed a million weeds, discovered muscles I never learned about in biology, and blistered my delicate hands.

When the bush beans were ready, I uprooted the entire plants, then hauled them to the edge of the garden where I'd plopped my lawn chair in the shade of a maple tree. I wanted to make this task as easy as possible. Kev saw me wiping sweat from my eyes with my dirty gloves. Soon he was beside me, expertly pulling beans from vines and tossing them into sacks.

"I thought you didn't like gardening," I said.

He grinned. "I don't. But I like you, and I like fresh beans."

Our pain and calluses proved worth it the first Sunday I brought tomatoes and beans to share. As people filled their bags in the church vestibule, Stan burst with pride, his wrinkled hand around my shoulder, his gray eyes dancing.

"I taught her everything she knows," he said, then laughed his way out the door.

I wondered how many tables had backaches after being loaded with all he'd grown. How many families had benefitted from the knowledge he so readily shared? Now he was passing his skill along to me. And sharing in the joy of my harvest.

We often don't realize the lives we impact by the seeds we plant in God's garden. Week after week, we share the Gospel, listen to problems, pray, and give words of encouragement. We wonder if the blisters on our hearts and headaches of misunderstanding are worth the meager fruit we can see.

Still, we refuse to give up, believing that one day soon the Master Gardener will put His arm around our shoulders, beaming with joy in our accomplishments for His sake. As He introduces us to the bounty of souls we've helped to grow, and they thank us for planting God's Word in their lives, we'll say with delight, "He taught me everything I know."

Two Scoops & a Sprinkle

❖ If we're tempted to give up—which can be daily—it's okay to ask the Lord to show us some of the fruit from our planting.

❖ Our job is to plant and pray. God waters the seeds and gives the harvest.

❖ Keeping a "Victory File" of notes and cards of thanks is a great way to remind ourselves that we are bearing fruit.

Dangerous Donuts

"Do not judge or you too will be judged. For in the same way you judge others, you will be judged, and with the measure you use, it will be measured to you"
(Matthew 7:1-2 NIV).

"Honey, come quick," I shrieked to Kevin. "That couple in the car across the road is in trouble!"

Standing at the picture window in our living room, I clamped both hands over my mouth to keep from sobbing. My heart hammered in fear, a contrast to the serene blanket of snow on the lawn.

When we relocated from Los Angeles to Paris, Illinois, three months earlier to pastor a rural church, we were surprised at the differences in culture. The stores displayed *Udder Balm* at the checkout counter in place of breath mints. Gas stations sold *live bait* and *mulch* right alongside the antifreeze. People waved as we passed their tractors on the highway and spoke to us at the farmers' market, even though we were strangers.

But no kind greeting or wave could have prepared us for the harrowing scene taking place before us now. This was culture shock at its worst.

Careening out of control just fifty yards from our house, the car was a flash of red and silver atop the frosty ground. Our eyes stayed frozen to the window for several seconds, watching the horror unfold. But, what could we do? All of our urban savoir faire was worthless to this couple, spinning on the snow like a child's top. I grabbed the only weapon I knew how to use, and bawled out a prayer. *"Lord, deliver those people,"* I shouted. *"They need your help right now, before they die, or flip onto the highway and hurt some—"*

Kevin placed a hand on my arm, interrupting my hysteria. "Wait, Jeanette. Look over there, opposite from the car. There's another one spinning in circles, going the reverse direction. I wonder if they could be doing that on purpose. Do you think it's some sort of winter game they play around here?"

Squinting to focus, I realized he was right. The cars faced each other, revolving in opposite directions, like two steel monsters dancing to the music of "Winter Wonderland." For several minutes they whirled, grinding their tires into the gravel. Picking up speed, their chrome bumpers reflected light from the pristine ground cover. When they'd reduced the snow to a slushy rut, they paused. The drivers appeared to sigh in contentment. And then off they blazed, disappearing down the highway, leaving us to stare at each other, befuddled.

The following morning, I worked for several hours before I gathered courage to ask my co-worker what we'd seen the day before. I certainly didn't want her to discover how dumb we city transplants were. She made it easy for me by reading my thoughts.

"You live six miles south of town, don't you? I bet you get a lot of teenagers coming out your way after it snows, doing *donuts*. It's safer out there, away from the highway," she explained.

I shook my head and grinned. "That's what you call it? *Donuts?*"

"Yeah." She chuckled. "Young people do it for fun when there's a good snow. It's pretty harmless. Just our method of keeping the boredom away during a long winter. I should have warned you about it. If someone from the city saw that for the first time, it might scare the stuffing out of them!"

"Yeah, it just might," I replied, trying to sound nonchalant. Later on, I told her about my panic in front of the picture window. To her credit, she didn't even laugh at me.

Since that first winter's excitement eleven years ago, I believe Kevin and I have adjusted well to rural living. We buy our mulch at the Speedy Fuel and say "hello" to people we've never met. But, I may never get used to donuts in the snow, rather than in my coffee.

Two Scoops & a Sprinkle

❖ Although we may not understand why people act the way they do, we're only called to love them, not figure them out.

❖ I believe the Lord honored my prayer of protection for those teens, even though it was rooted in panic. But I'll bet He laughed as He sent the angels out!

❖ I'm thankful my friend at work didn't make fun of me when I told her my story. I couldn't help it that I'd never heard of the country version of donuts. She endeared herself to me by her kindness.

From Outlaws to God's Kids

"In him we have redemption though his blood, the forgiveness of sins, in accordance with the riches of God's grace" **(Ephesians 1:7 NIV).**

My husband and I have a friend named Jesse James, with a twin brother named Frank. No joke. Kevin met him at a men's Bible study. Apart from his name, Jesse doesn't resemble the notorious train robber of the nineteenth century. But his four-year-old grandson, Lucas, may be trying to get by with a little outlaw spirit in his own way.

In his preschool class this year, he'd heard the story of a boy who'd received nothing but coal in his stocking. Lucas knew Santa rewarded good boys and girls, but now he was worried. What if he hadn't measured up to Santa's standards? Would his stocking, as well as the huge, glistening gift box under the tree, be stuffed with black lumps?

His heart pounded and his usually nimble fingers trembled as he opened each gift in his stocking. Candy. Hot Wheels. Erasable crayons. More candy. Whew. That wasn't so bad.

Now, to see what the package under the tree contained. In spite of his self-doubt, Lucas ripped away the sparkling red paper to reveal . . . a battery-powered indoor four-wheeler, the #1 request on his wish list. A sigh of relief tumbled from his lips.

Collapsing on the floor, Lucas hugged his belly and laughed, his gingerbread eyes dancing with the tree lights. His baby sister crawled over to join him in the giggling, even though she had no idea why they were laughing.

"What are you hooting about?" asked his mom.

"Because it's so funny."

"What's so funny, Lucas?"

Climbing aboard the four-wheeler, he giggled some more and said, "I was bad this year, and I still got really good stuff!"

Although Lucas thought he'd put one over on Santa, we can take a lesson about God's grace from him. None of us deserves the gifts He gives.

I bet you've heard this verse from Romans: "All have sinned and fall short of the glory of God" (Romans 3:23 *NIV*). Have you read the verse that follows it? "God did it for us. Out of sheer generosity, he put us in right standing with himself. A pure gift. He got us out of the mess we're in and restored us to where he always wanted us to be. And he did it by means of Jesus Christ" (Romans 3:24 *The Message*).

God has already taken care of the sin problem by accepting

Jesus' blood sacrifice in our place. Just as Lucas couldn't measure up to the standard of perfection he thought Santa required, we can't measure up to God's standard of perfection. We simply open the package of His love by admitting we cannot save ourselves. Then, in spite of our self-doubt, we ask Him to step in and take over our lives.

That's when He changes us from outlaws to loving citizens of His kingdom. It's His best gift, wrapped in the sparkling package of a man named Jesus. He calls it grace, and it sure beats a sock full of hard black stuff.

Two Scoops & a Sprinkle

❖ Although no one gets away with sin, God doesn't even the score the same way we do. He's already punished Jesus in our place. Believing that makes those who love Him want to quit sinning.

❖ Just as Lucas delighted in receiving good stuff in spite of his poor behavior, we should delight in God's favor. His grace is not a license to sin, but a reminder of His goodness and the power to vanquish sin. The more we embrace His grace, the more we'll long to please Him.

❖ We not only need grace to enter God's family, we need it moment by moment to live strong, godly lives. The power of the Holy Spirit changes us from outlaws to overcomers.

Who Are You Laughing At?

"Our mouths were filled with laughter, our tongues with songs of joy"
(Psalm 126:2 NIV).

"Jesus loves the little children, all the children of the world."
With my squeaky soprano dancing to the peeling paint on the
ceiling, I sang with the abandon of the seven-year-old that I was.
I didn't leave out a single vacation Bible school song from my
concert of one that day. "Jesus Loves Me," "Deep and Wide,"
"The Wise Man Built His House Upon the Rock," and "The
B-I-B-L-E" filled my heart with joy and the air of the Burbank
Beauty College with music.

Nearly every lady who passed by me grinned or waved as I
warbled the hour away. Because I couldn't hear a scrap from the
moment the stylist lowered that huge dryer bonnet over my red
locks, I assumed no one else could hear me, either. I interpreted
the smiles and waves as endearing gestures to a cute little girl,

nothing more. Bored and hot under the dryer, and not old enough to read *Ladies Home Journal*, I decided to serenade myself. Or so I thought.

On the third verse of "The Wise Man Built His House upon the Rock," the stylist came to check my hair. He tilted the bonnet back, and I stopped abruptly when I suddenly realized that I'd been performing for the entire salon. When he guided me into a chair and twirled me around to the huge mirror, my face looked back at me, as red and hot as my hair.

That was several decades ago, and the beginning of my painful career of fretting over what "they" would think of me. For too long I tried too hard to impress people, rather than simply accepting myself and enjoying my unique personality.

Our loving Heavenly Father wants us to be confident. Confident people can laugh at themselves. Their faces don't turn red when they sing too loud, can't read or garden as well as their neighbor, or aren't athletic. Confident people readily admit their faults, and can even discuss them without fearing what others think. Their self-expectations are realistic because they look at things from God's perspective. They know it's okay with God that their performance is not yet perfect.

The Lord isn't shocked with the dumb things we do or say. That's one reason He put His Spirit in us—to make up for what we lack. If we focus on every deficiency and mistake, we'll never receive the grace He wants to give us, grace that will help us grow.

If we're constantly trying to impress people, we will live

nervous, self-conscious lives rather than relaxing in God's love and acceptance. This doesn't mean we have a haughty, "take me or leave me" attitude that bulldozes over others' feelings or wishes. It simply means we don't take ourselves too seriously. Most people focus far more on their own lives and problems than they do ours. If we make a stupid blunder, they don't notice it, or it simply makes them feel better that they're not the only imperfect ones. Many times, I have jokingly said after doing something ditzy, "Oh, I did that on purpose, so the rest of you wouldn't feel bad when you act crazy."

Accept who you are with grace, be confident, and seek your Father's approval more than people's applause. Learn to laugh at yourself.

Now, would you like to join me in a few verses of "Deep and Wide?"

Two Scoops & a Sprinkle

❖ Kids must be taught to care what others think of them. Perhaps when Jesus told us to be like children, one quality He had in mind was their oblivion to approval from others.

❖ Laughing at ourselves not only relieves stress, it helps set us free from pride.

❖ Although God is perfect, He is not a perfectionist. He doesn't expect us to behave perfectly, only to trust and obey Him.

Wrinkles and All

"'The Lord does not look at the things man looks at. Man looks at the outward appearance, but the Lord looks at the heart'"
(I Samuel 16:7 NIV).

Do you rejoice if you remember what errand brought you from the den to the kitchen? Instead of planning trips to Greece or Spain, do you shout "hallelujah!" for a trip to Dairy Queen? And do you fidget in your seat when they want you to blow out the candles on your birthday cake because you just want to cut it and get to the sugar high?

That's okay. We're allowed to not be as young as we once were. In fact, it's natural.

We live in a society obsessed with youth—faces devoid of wrinkles or blemishes, bodies with no bulges or cellulite, and brains that can zing an answer before you finish the question. Isn't the idea that youth is better than age a mirage?

267

What's so appealing about wrinkle-less but pimple-full faces? Or bodies devoid of cellulite, but raging with hormones? And what use is a quick answer when the question is, "Can you give me some money to buy a new cell phone?"

As Kevin stood talking to me while I applied goop to my face one night, he asked, "What are you putting on now?"

"Deep wrinkle repair cream."

"You don't have any deep wrinkles," he said.

I pointed. "See these motorcycle ruts in my upper lip? These are definitely deep wrinkles."

He stepped closer and squinted. "Oh, I hadn't noticed them."

"Thanks for saying that. Did you not notice my bulging belly, either? I've gone up two pant sizes in the last year. Whenever I go clothes shopping these days, I just head for the hippo-size rack. It's discouraging." I sighed real loud, so he'd feel extra sorry for me.

It worked. "I'm sorry, hon. That's rough. But I really hadn't noticed either of those things. I just love you for the fun, interesting person you are."

Wow. He hadn't noticed them. Could that be because he hasn't been looking for wrinkles? He's been looking for all the things that make our marriage great: companionship, fun, understanding.

I suddenly realized what a hypocrite I'd been. I criticize society for dwelling too much on youth, and then I fret over wrinkles, a thickening middle, gray hair, and knees that pop at odd moments.

Shouldn't I be more like Kevin . . . and Jesus, who don't notice all the flaws in others?

What makes us think God sits on His throne with a huge magnifying glass, inspecting us for faults? Why is it easier for us to accept the correction of the Lord when we have messed up, than to accept His hoorays when we have done something right? God is proud of you simply for being His child.

When we get to Heaven, the Father won't be waiting with a huge book chronicling all the wrinkles in our lives so He can rebuke us. The only book He'll read is the Lamb's Book of Life, in which He's written the names of those who have accepted His blood sacrifice for them. And all He will say as He reads your name is, "Well done, good and faithful servant...enter into the joy of your lord" (Matthew 25:23, *NKJV*).

From now on, I'm going to tweak my thinking to mirror the Master's. I'm accepting myself and others, wrinkles and all, and focusing on what really counts—a person's heart.

Two Scoops & a Sprinkle

❖ If you find it easier to criticize yourself than to be comfortable with yourself, ask the Lord or a friend to point out some of your most likable traits.

❖ God's "well done, good and faithful servant" when we reach Heaven won't be based on our perfect performance, but our position in Christ.

❖ We make better spouses and friends when we notice and compliment the good in others rather than their flaws.

Just Give Me a Kiss

"Then they asked him, 'What must we do to do the works God requires?' Jesus answered, 'The work of God is this: to believe in the one he has sent'"

(John 6:28 NIV).

When our children were tiny, neither of them could pronounce the letter "L." Esther said it like a "Y" so that "I like you" came out "I yike you." Ron's sounded like "W" where "pillow" turned into "piwwow." It was especially amusing when Esther was five and Ron was two, because neither had yet outgrown this little impediment.

One afternoon I paused from a book I was reading and asked, "Who wants to give Mommy a kiss?"

"A kiss on the yips?" said Estie.

Ron hotly corrected, "Not the yips, the wips!"

"Someone just give me a kiss!" I laughed.

I wonder how often I behave the same way toward God. He

says, "Talk to me, please." I argue, "Right here, in the middle of Wal-Mart? Can't I at least wait 'til I get in the car, or home?"

He asks, "Do a favor for that person who treated you nasty." I argue, "And let them hurt me again?" As if God doesn't know them, and I can't trust Him to keep me safe or heal my hurt.

He tells me, "Just relax." I want to make a list of forty-seven ways to relax, and then check them off as I accomplish them.

Every year, bookstores sell millions of books on "how to live the Christian life." Such books can be helpful. They can also confuse us, if the messages contradict each other or have so many steps to success that we feel overwhelmed.

The Bible is not a list of do's and don't's. It is a roadmap to eternal life, a comfort in stress and sorrow, and a handbook for successful living. If we turn it into merely a rulebook, it appears harsh and demanding. After a while, we conclude that God is harsh and demanding, too. If we don't memorize a verse each day or bow our heads while praying, we might think we're displeasing God. Then when He says, "Give me a kiss," we strive to learn how to pronounce it correctly and where to plant it.

Someone once asked Jesus, "What must I do to work the works of God?" His answer still shocks us: "Believe on me, because I am the One sent from God."

What? No do-do-doing stuff to impress God? Just trust in Jesus? Can it be that simple?

Of course it can. If you love someone, you will want to make them happy. Spending time with them, just getting to know each other, will come naturally. You don't need them to fill out a questionnaire on what color tissues they like to blow their nose on, how many pickles they prefer on their sandwich, and what order they go on the rides at Disney World. That would subtract all the joy from your relationship.

God doesn't search for achievers. What He's looking for are believers. A few good men, women, boys, and girls who will trust Him enough to place their entire life in His hands. To go where He says go, to have faith in His love, and to believe His Word even when situations look hopeless.

It's called faith. And it's just the kind of kiss God is asking us to give Him.

Two Scoops & a Sprinkle

❖ The more complicated a system of belief is, the more men's ideas are undergirding it. God simplifies life for us by requiring shockingly few actions on our part.

❖ If salvation were mostly dependent upon our works and very little dependent upon God, we'd have reason to boast. But it's not, and we don't.

❖ Grace means trusting God not only to save you, but to help you walk with Him in victory.

Leave Yourself Alone

"Who is he that condemns? Christ Jesus, who died—
more than that, who was raised to life—is at the right
hand of God and is also interceding for us"
(Romans 8:34 NIV).

"I read all the books you got me for Christmas," said our four-year-old granddaughter Jenessa. "Then Mommy took me to the widawary to get some more books."

Hmm. . . . "Oh, the library," I finally answered. "That's a hard word to say, isn't it?"

"Well, yes, but widawary isn't hard!" Jenessa had solved her little dilemma without realizing how amusing—and wise—she was acting.

Her younger brother Daniel was three when we drove by a new auto parts store on our way to take the kids shopping. "Have you been in the new Hearty Wheels store?" I asked Kevin.

"No, I haven't."

From his safety seat in the back, Daniel piped, "I have!" We wondered how he'd managed that little miracle.

A few years later, when their baby sister Alyssa was 2 1/2, we sat down to watch a movie. Because she'd not finished her lunch, her mommy made her stay at the table. When we noticed a puddle of water in front of her and ran to fetch a towel, she said in a flat, innocent tone, "Something happened."

We don't mind when these little people mispronounce words or act silly. Knowing they aren't capable of conducting themselves like adults, we don't expect it of them. We make allowances, letting them behave like the children they are. We even laugh at their antics.

Do you suppose God is any less loving than we are? Do you imagine He gets disgusted when we make mistakes, even the same mistake day after day? Are you afraid that you are a disappointment to Him and He's sorry He let you into His family?

Ask me how I know. The devil tells me those same lies.

God knows you won't be mature until you see Jesus face to face. Because of that, He makes allowances for your blunders and failures. He's not frustrated with you because you aren't flawless. He may even laugh at some of the silly things you do and say.

Please don't misunderstand. God wants you to grow up and respond to people and situations in a mature manner. It just doesn't ruin His day like you might think when you don't perform perfectly every time. He's a realist, not a perfectionist.

Why don't you leave yourself alone? Don't be depressed when you have failed to live up to your own unrealistic expectations of how a mature Christian should act. You aren't helping yourself grow when you can't allow some occasional blunders and faults. You're a lot more fun to be around when you leave yourself alone.

When we are able to relax and accept God's unconditional love, His mercy covers our imperfections, causing us to mature beyond our limits. Because we are able to forgive and like ourselves in spite of a few imperfections, God's grace moves in and empowers us to excel like never before.

Let God's grace change you if you need to be changed, and don't be your own aristarch. And if you want to know what that word means, you'll have to go to the widawary.

Two Scoops & a Sprinkle

❖ Because our modern society focuses on self and appearances, we can succumb to the temptation to dwell on our imperfections more than our victories. God is the opposite. His book of lists contains every time we obeyed, but none of the failures.

❖ When Jesus said, "Forgive those who sin against you," He meant us too. We can learn to forgive ourselves and go on with life, knowing that the Lord has wiped our slate clean.

❖ God's grace is never a license to continue sinning. But the more we focus on His kindness and love, the more we want to please Him by following His hand of guidance.

Not My Thought

"We use our powerful God-tools for smashing warped philosophies, tearing down barriers erected against the truth of God, fitting every loose thought and emotion and mpulse into the structure of life shaped by Christ"
(2 Corinthians 10:5 The Message).

When a fellow minister wanted to teach his three-year-old daughter to resist temptation, he brought it down to her level. "When the devil puts a thought into your mind to disobey Mommy or Daddy, be mean to your brother, or throw a tantrum, just put your hands on your hips and say, 'That's not my thought!' Then the devil will leave you alone."

The next day, the pastor walked into his daughter's room. Toys and clothes covered the floor, the bed, and the dresser. "Stacie, this room is a mess. C'mon, now, let's clean it up."

Stacie quickly put her hands on her hips, looked Daddy in the eyes, and declared, "That's not my thought!"

Although directed at the wrong person, Stacie had the right idea. She recognized that wicked thoughts originated from outside herself, and she resisted them at once. Stacie's story defies the idea that we ourselves conjure up negative thoughts, when in fact the devil plants them in our mind. Our job? Use Scripture to boot them out of our brain.

When I've used Stacie's method of defying the devil's thoughts, I've had great success. Here are some thoughts I've booted out.

"I am so stupid. Why can't I do anything right?" (self-condemnation)

"I don't understand him/her. If I were them, I never would have . . ." (judgmentalism)

"_____ doesn't care about me. If he did, he wouldn't have acted that way." (self-pity)

"What am I going to do? Why isn't God working on this problem as fast and neatly as I need?" (worry)

"This issue (or person) is never going to change. We may as well just learn to live with it." (doubt)

"I don't see how we'll ever be able to afford our own home. We'll probably have to go live in a senior citizen's housing unit for poor people when we retire." (distrust)

Can you relate to any of these? Not one of them is our thought. All are foreign ideas, coming from the enemy of our souls, Satan himself. Once we are born again, we receive the very nature and mind of God (I Corinthians 2:16), who is love personified. If a thought enters our mind that is anything but love, we know its source is Satan, and need to confront him with the authority given us by Jesus (Luke 10:19).

Because our feelings and attitudes follow our thoughts, it is essential that we take every thought captive to the authority of Jesus. Often that requires speaking to the thought aloud, even with our hands on our hips, as if rebuking Satan himself, because we are. We must be bold and aggressive when it involves the devil infiltrating our minds. He doesn't fight fair. The weapon we overpower him with is the Bible, contradicting his foreign messages with God's Word. Speak a Scripture or sing a biblical song to overcome those thoughts and gain victory over Satan, and to help you live the full, positive life Jesus promised in John 10:10.

I'd better go now, in case Kevin is thinking of taking me out to eat. . . . *Now,* that's *my thought.*

Two Scoops & a Sprinkle

❖ Satan disguises his thoughts as ours, planting "I" statements in our minds: "I am so depressed today;" "I can't do anything right," etc. When we recognize their source, we can kick them out with the Word of God and praise.

❖ Sometimes the enemy uses others to plant his thoughts in our minds. Although we wouldn't shout, "That's not my thought!" in their face, we can still reject it by not acting upon it.

❖ The devil can use Scripture twisted wrongly to deceive us, just as he tried to do with Jesus in the desert. The more we know God's Word, the better we are at overcoming the devil's lies.

A Pitiful Slice of Pie

*"Don't you know that a little yeast works through the
whole batch of dough?"*
(1 Corinthians 5:6 NIV).

At the pie social after evening church service, I chatted with
everyone at our table. Except Red. Every time I looked his way
and started to talk, I noticed he had his napkin to his mouth, an
intense look in his eyes. I wondered what the problem was.

As we were clearing our plates, he finally put his napkin

down and said, "How many pits do you think I found in my slice of cherry pie tonight?"

I lifted my eyebrows and hesitated a minute. Was he teasing me? "Zero, I hope."

He grinned in triumph and said, "Nope. Twenty-eight!"

My bottom lip slid to my knees when he described piling one pit after another onto his plate at the church social. Either Aunt Josephine forgot to pit the cherries before she baked that pie, or the factory's pitting machine malfunctioned the day those babies were canned.

I was amazed and relieved Red hadn't broken a tooth after biting so many pits. I was also impressed with his tenacity, sticking with that rocky dessert to the last crust. Perhaps he kept hoping it would improve. Or maybe he got enthused about counting the pits to see how many someone could pack into one slice of pie.

Little things can make a huge difference. Did the young boy in Luke 9 realize what an immense impact his five biscuits and two sardines made in thousands of lives? What an enormous relief the woman caught in adultery must have experienced when Jesus spoke two little sentences: "Neither do I condemn you. Go and sin no more." And the thief on the cross next to the Master must still be rejoicing at this little sentence: "Today you will be with me in Paradise."

I've been pondering what things in my life I could vastly improve by a simple, little adjustment. . . .

What if, instead of worrying about a situation I can't change,

I said a little prayer that God would mend it?

What if I talked a little less and listened a little more?

What if, instead of being sarcastic when my husband steps on my feelings, I gave myself a little time to cool down?

What if I ate a little less food each day, or exercised a few minutes longer?

What if I gave a little more money to the Lord and a little more time to my family?

I could give more little compliments, or write a short note to someone who needs an ounce of support. I could go a bit out of my way to visit someone who's lonesome. I could mend a wee tear in a broken relationship, and speak a small word of kindness and grace.

I could gripe a tad less, and thank a bit more. I could spend a smidgen less time talking about what I dislike about situations, and spend a little more time praying for God to help people and change nations.

I could think slightly less of me, myself, and I, and a lot more of you and your needs.

We all make a bigger difference than we think. Our little words, thoughts, and actions matter more than we realize. Just as Red's pitiful pie was not too enjoyable, neither would the world be very sweet without all the little—make that big—things we do.

Two Scoops & a Sprinkle

❖ We can avoid the breakdown of relationships by not speaking the first mean little word that pops into our minds. We can say a small prayer instead, that God would help us understand the other's point of view.

❖ It's amazing how a tiny compliment or smile can turn someone's day from gloom to gleam.

❖ Even little thoughts of faith and hope can lead our heart out of despair and into hope.

No Charge

"For if by the one man's offense death reigned through the one,
much more those who receive abundance of grace
and of the gift of righteousness will reign in
life through the one, Jesus Christ"
(Romans 5:17 NKJV).

"I'm not taking my shoes off!" I muttered through clenched teeth as we stood in line waiting to pass through airport security. "It's outrageous to expect everyone here to remove their shoes. No wonder this line is taking a decade!"

I knew it had been several years since we'd flown, and the regulations had tightened since 9/11, but *shoes? Come on.*

In spite of my undercover spunk, I acquiesced to the security guard when he told me I'd have to remove my tennies. *Oh well,* I thought. *I have nothing to hide, and it's worth the trouble and time to know they are keeping us safe.* By the time we reached our gate, I was a less ruffled flyer.

When we found our seats on the plane, the flight attendants began their ream of announcements. I'd known the safety instructions since I was a child, so I sat politely and listened. But when I heard, "You may purchase a box snack for a charge of $5.00. Please see examples on page seventy-six of your Expensive Sky Magazine," I came unglued. Again.

"What? They are charging for food on planes now? We've never had to pay for food on a plane, and I've been flying since I was nine years old, when the stewardesses wore bright orange hats and go-go boots! I refuse to buy food on a plane."

Kevin, usually the thrifty one, had switched roles with me and became Mr. Magnanimous. "I'll buy you a meal if you want, honey. I don't mind. Are you hungry?" He opened his wallet, offering me a five.

"It doesn't matter if I'm hungry, Kev. It's the principle of the thing. I will not spend your hard-earned money to pay for food on an airplane. Just look at these pictures of their box meals: gummy candies in the shape of planes, juice in a box, a smattering of crackers, and something that vaguely resembles cheese. Keep your money or spend it on something better than this Barbie meal. I have almonds in my purse and trail mix and chocolate in my carry-on bag. I'll be fine till we get to Portland." I shoved his hand back into his lap then trudged through my purse, hunting for almonds.

I don't consider myself old. Certainly not old enough to start resisting change in a major way. So, why all the fuss? Why did I put on my cranky pants over this minor irritation? Was I riled because they are now charging for something they'd previously given away? And even though I realize my forty-plus years' worth of airline meals were not truly free, at least they appeared to be. They'd hidden them in the price of the ticket, a method I obviously found more comfortable.

I'm relieved God doesn't operate on the same basis as the airlines. He's always freely given us His love. God is never going to change the plan and start charging us to become members of His family.

Two thousand years ago, Jesus shed His sinless blood so all mankind could know God as Father. When He said in Romans 10, "Whosoever will, may come," He meant it. Not just for that week or that millennium, but for all time. Salvation is forever free.

I'm proud to fly with a Pilot who can be trusted to keep His word. If God says "no charge," it will always be "no charge." Now, that's the ticket.

Two Scoops & a Sprinkle

❖ Jesus' blood has always been enough to erase every sin of every person. If I am trying to make up for my sin by penance, or earning God's favors by being good enough, I misunderstand His grace. Free means free. He has already paid for me.

❖ Grace is one of the most challenging concepts to convince people to receive. Some think it's a license to sin. Others can't grasp that God wouldn't require anything in return for His love. Romans and Galatians are excellent resources for explaining grace to non-believers or baby Christians.

❖ "Be prepared" works not only for the Boy Scouts, but also for flyers. I keep plenty of snacks in my carry-on bag when I fly, so I don't have to pay excessive prices for airline food.

The Rest of Your Life

"'Assuredly, I say to you, unless you are converted and become
as little children, you will by no means
enter the kingdom of heaven'"
(Matthew 18:3 NKJV).

My daddy was an affable, compassionate, fun-loving guy. His brown eyes crinkled and danced when he laughed, which was often. Uncle Jack once told me that Daddy would give his last dime to someone who needed it. He was also an alcoholic, and died when he was thirty-eight of cirrhosis of the liver. I was barely ten.

Daddy's death filled me with rage. I was mad at Daddy for leaving me. I was mad at Mom for divorcing him when I was six and marrying another alcoholic. And I was mad at God for what I thought was His decision to wrench Daddy away from me when I needed him most, right before my teen years.

"You could have prevented my daddy from dying, Lord. He was a Christian, after all. I know lots of Christians who do worse things than drinking. He was such a gentle, sweet man. I don't understand."

I wore myself out trying to answer my own questions. As a teenager, I followed pursuits that allowed me to create attention for myself, such as singing and drama. I rebelled against authority, trying to fill my empty emotional cup with anything that might resemble the daddy-love I craved. None of my attempts worked.

Only after seeing the dark-to-light change in my stepdad after his conversion did I realize that Jesus was Who I'd been searching for all those years. He alone could fill in the gaps that Daddy's death had left in my soul. I invited Him to.

Shortly after I married Kevin, he took me to visit Daddy's grave, which I'd never seen. Standing by the headstone, tears dripping down my chin, a shaft of insight penetrated my thoughts. *Perhaps it was best that Daddy went when he did. What if he had lived, and ended up hurting someone? Our family's suffering over his alcoholism has made me compassionate toward those who have alcoholic parents. I can understand others' grief when someone dear to them dies or abandons them. I wouldn't be this strong and empathetic if it wasn't for Daddy's death.*

Finally, I was free to accept Daddy's passing, even if I didn't understand it.

I never will be happy he died. Not for a moment do I believe it was God's will. I think Daddy could have lived a productive, joyful life if he'd made wiser choices. But I have peace about it now. And I'm not wasting time trying to find someone to blame.

However, there've been some other events in my life that I've never understood, no matter how much I tied my brain into knots. I've concluded that I may never know why certain things took place. For my own sanity, I've given them over to God's loving care, in spite of unanswered questions.

Are there issues in your life that have upset you and caused you to doubt God's love or wisdom? Would your loved one still be here, would you have that job you wanted, or not ended up in trouble if only . . . ?

May I tell you something, dear one? *You may never know.* You only torture yourself by asking a thousand why's. You will never be able to rest and fully believe the love of God until you accept that you don't have all the answers, but the One who loves you best can be trusted to heal your hurts.

Then sink back to rest in His love, for the rest of your life.

Two Scoops & a Sprinkle

❖ We love to fit everything in our lives into neat little compartments, so we'll feel we are in charge. Let's not fool ourselves into thinking we are capable of running our own lives. The sooner we give God charge and allow Him to lead, the sooner we'll find the peace we crave.

❖ Death is a thief. Death was not a part of Eden's landscape, and it won't be in heaven. I look forward to the day when Jesus will finally put death to death forever.

❖ Children more easily trust than grown-ups do. They believe everything they're told without reservations. When we choose to trust God in spite of unanswered questions, we are obeying Jesus' command to become like little children.

Thank You for Changing my Destiny:

Mom, when you said, "I always wanted you."

Esther, when you said, "Mom, you're not ditzy. You are one of the wisest people I know."

Ron, when you said, "You're gonna be doing something for the next ten years anyway, why not write a book?"

Ned Jenison, when you said, "Yes, we'd like to do your column."

Clella Camp, when you said, "You need to go to a writers conference."

Cammie Quinn, when you said, "You're a master at humor."

Jim Watkins, when you said, "I can use this. Can you cut it from 800 words to 300?"

Diana Flegal, when you said, "I'd like to represent you at Hartline Literary."

Lin Johnson, when you said, "You are one of my success stories."

Patti Lacy, when you said, "Will you come to my writers group?"

Tammy Barley and Patti Lacy when you said, "Yes" to making my words shine brighter than they did before.

Rhonda Schrock, when you said, "Can we meet?"

Susan Reinhardt, when you said, "I'm in this for the long haul. And you?"

Stacey Graham, when you said "yes" to inducting me into An Army of Ermas.

Diane Estrella, Bridgett Trover, Terri Tiffany, Cecelia Lester, and Amy McGilvery, when you said "yes" to reading your brains out and helping me choose the chapters for this book.

The lovely people of Paris, Illinois, and the sheep at Nevins Christian Church, when you said, "Welcome. You belong here."

Tonya, Betty, Lou Ann, & Angel, when you said, "We're so glad you came." You guys are my best cheerleaders.

My readers, when you said, "I believe in you." I love hearing from you. Please contact me at jeanettelevellie@gmail.com, www.jeanettelevellie.com, Facebook, or Twitter.